AMERICAN
FOLK
TOYS

AMERICAN
FOLK
TOYS

EASY-TO-BUILD TOYS
FOR KIDS OF ALL AGES

JOHN R. NELSON, JR.

The Taunton Press

Cover photo: Boyd Hagen
Back-cover photos : Stan Sherer

BOOKS & VIDEOS

for fellow enthusiasts

Text © 1998 by John R. Nelson, Jr.
Photos © 1998 by The Taunton Press, Inc., except where noted
Illustrations © 1998 by The Taunton Press, Inc.

Printed in the United States of America
10 9 8 7 6 5 4 3 2 1

The Taunton Press, Inc., 63 South Main Street,
PO Box 5506, Newtown, CT 06470-5506
e-mail: tp@taunton.com

Library of Congress Cataloging-in-Publication Data

Nelson, John R.
        American folk toys / John R. Nelson, Jr.
           p.   cm.
        ISBN 1-56158-221-2
        1. Wooden toy making.   2. Wooden toys — United States.   I. Title.
TT174.5.W6N46   1997   97-46760
745.592 — dc21   CIP

About Your Safety

Working wood is inherently dangerous. Using hand or power tools improperly or ignoring standard safety practices can lead to permanent injury or even death. Don't try to perform operations you learn about here (or elsewhere) unless you're certain they are safe for you. If something about an operation doesn't feel right, don't do it. Look for another way. We want you to enjoy the craft, so please keep safety foremost in your mind whenever you're in the shop.

To my children, Kristin Erika, John Eric, Martha Jeanne, Seth Peter, and Paul Marius, and my grandchildren, Krystle and Sarah — you have taught me that, truly, children are the carriers of life!

Acknowledgments

More people helped me with this book in more ways than I can possibly recognize here. I owe thanks to many persons whose names I cannot remember, who over the last 25 years told me about folk toys they'd played with as children—and sometimes were able to find and demonstrate for me. This was long before I thought of writing a book about toys, but these people made clear to me how important folk toys had been to them and their families.

But many other collectors, shopkeepers, museum personnel, and proud owners came along later, when I began developing this book, to whom I would like to express my gratitude specifically. Arnold Friedmann, Professor Emeritus of Art at the University of Massachusetts, was most generous in sharing his marvelous collection of balancing toys with me; George Pratt of the Hadley Farm Museum showed me two beautiful examples of folk toys in a huge barn full of everything from churns to carriages; Larry Lefkowitz brought me some of his favorite toys from New Jersey and introduced me to Will-o'-the-Wisp; Aldith Allen and

Suzanne Flynt of the Memorial Hall Museum, Old Deerfield, Massachusetts, found several priceless dolls for me to have photographed; Jean Rees and Marianna Campbell of the Peabody Essex Museum, Salem, Massachusetts, were helpful in tracking down images of 19th-century folk toys; the Webb Museum of American Folk Art in Shelburne, Vermont, and Old Sturbridge Village in Sturbridge, Massachusetts, were also obliging in providing examples of folk art and folk toys.

Joseph Hickerson of the Smithsonian Institution, Washington, shared his extensive bibliography of folk art with me, and Edla Holm, Richard Davis, Joyce Merriam, and Melinda McIntosh of the DuBois Library, University of Massachusetts, helped me locate photographs, drawings, and etymologies; thanks also to the staffs of the Boston Public Library and the Jones and Monson Memorial libraries, Amherst, Massachusetts. Jill Burns of the Worcester (Massachusetts) Art Museum was very accommodating in providing images of Puritan America.

Moosehead Traders of Greenville, Maine, and Hamilton Antiques of Moosehead Lake, Maine, were helpful in locating historical materials, as was Kay Baker of Kay Baker Antiques, Amherst,

Massachusetts. Additional thanks are due to my University of Massachusetts colleagues Peggy O'Brien of Irish Studies, for help with the history of the limberjack; Ron Welburn, Native American Studies, for his knowledge of Native American toys; Audrey Duckert and Kirby Farrell, English Department, for etymological assistance with the shoofly rocking horse and information on the history of childhood, respectively; Gary Aho, Professor Emeritus of Medieval Literature, who set me straight about some incorrect toy scholarship by translating from Old Icelandic parts of the *Grettis Saga;* and Joyce Berkman, History Department, for bibliographic information on 17th- and 18th-century American family life.

Thanks also to Sylvia Snape, English MFA Secretary, University of Massachusetts, who loaned me several of her family's folk toys; Donald and Phyllis Hastings, who demonstrated a treasured marble roller still in vigorous use; and Bill and Dirk Jeffery, for their antique spinning top. Dermott Morley, of Leicester, Massachusetts, merits sincere appreciation for his assistance with the saltbox dollhouse. And thanks to Richard Hooke of Amherst, Massachusetts, who showed me how to cut model-sailboat sails using a hot nail.

My brother, Mark Nelson of Hillsboro, Oregon, a better carpenter and craftsman than I'll ever be, showed me some years ago how to make broad files; Scott Agne, of the local Leader Home Center, Amherst, was enthusiastic about each project and helped me find construction materials.

I'd also like to thank Bruce Wilcox of the University of Massachusetts Press, for his enthusiasm and counsel; Stan Sherer, photographer, whose talent and professionalism added greatly to the book's visual display of toy-making information; and Professor R. Bruce Hoadley of Wood Technology at the University of Massachusetts, a living encyclopedia of knowledge about wood. Rick Peters, Peter Chapman, and Joanne Renna of The Taunton Press were invaluable sources of support from the first days we worked together.

Lastly, I would like to extend heartfelt gratitude to my wife, Rennie McCluskey Nelson, and to my two youngest children, Seth Peter and Paul Marius Nelson, who patiently withheld criticism for long periods when it seemed my entire existence was consumed by the shop, the library, or the writing desk.

To all, thank you, thank you!

Contents

Introduction

After collecting and building American folk toys for 25 years, I'm convinced that the best American folk toys have soul.

What do I mean? Simply that compared to so many other varieties of playthings, American folk toys have a spirit, a wryness and humor, a comical or winsome quality, and a robustness that says, "reach out and touch me: give me a spin, a lift, a twist, a pull, a breeze, and I will connect with you." And that this connection does not diminish after a day, a week, or a year. They possess a particular vitality, sometimes mixed with rough genius, that makes them more than the sum of their parts. Dozens of people from whom I've collected American folk toy designs (their owners won't part with the originals) have told me the same story: "Thirty years after we gave that thing to the kids, they come back and play with it just as much as the grandchildren."

This book draws upon a significant but oft-forgotten tradition within American folk history—folk toys, which began delighting children over two centuries ago. Folk toys are simple, yet often very ingenious in design and operation. Most were invented or modified and made by men and women with few tools, little space and precious little money, to touch a child's imagination and fancy. In the period between 1800 and 1860, a working man might expect to earn something between 60 and 75 cents a day, and employment was by no means certain; each toy became a small triumph of innovation and industry.

But the toys in this book are also triumphs of American folk art, an increasingly recognized (and collected) aesthetic form in which the maker says, "I am determined not to go without art in my life; if I did not inherit it or cannot afford to buy it, I'll make it myself here and now out of the materials and with the tools at hand." Certainly part of the fortitude and charm of these toys lies in their mixture of unpretentiousness, latent determination, and economy in both design and material cost.

The toys in this collection are all very low-tech and most are disarmingly easy to make. Many of them run on gravity (the marble game, rolling acrobat, carousel), muscle power (the self-propelled sled, Flip the Acrobat, the whimmydiddle), or wind (the sailboat). There are no springs to break. And there's not a printed circuit, cheap electric motor, cold-soldered wire, or depleted battery pack in the lot. What's more, they have come to the present trailing behind a long history of successful and creative play; otherwise, most of them would never have been passed from generation to generation. They've also survived because a legacy of design improvements has made sure that they're rugged, if not almost indestructible. And that's not a bad pedigree.

What can you expect in making the folk toys in this book? You'll use the same hand tools folk makers used 150 years ago. There's nothing high-tech or complex about anything you need to cut out, assemble, or finish. A measuring tape, compass, adjustable square, carpenter's awl, handsaw, coping saw, hammer, hand drill with bits, screwdriver, plane, coarse file, jackknife, sandpaper, nontoxic paint, three sizes of paintbrushes, and a small, well-lighted workspace are all that's required to make most of the toys. If you wish to save money, I've included a brief section on buying good used tools in the text. And if you want to use two simple power tools, an electric drill and a saber-saw, I've included advice for buying them as well.

You'll continue a tradition of American folk art that began after the American Revolution and flourished, roughly, until the Civil War; you'll also preserve designs that have been passed down for generations and begin a tradition within your own family.

You'll also work in a form where you'll happily park your perfectionist tendencies at the door. Small glitches are common in the best folk art and make it all the more human.

And you'll create a unique toy of lasting delight for any child.

Try making several of these toys with simple tools, even if you have an elaborate workshop. Perhaps you'll discover unexpectedly, as I did, that it is pleasantly satisfying to fashion a human or animal or mechanical shape without the tension arising from razor-sharp carbide blades or knives or cutters whirling, and without the inescapable noise of power equipment. Meanwhile you'll discover (or rediscover!) some of the fundamental tool skills our not-so-distant ancestors demonstrated with such creativity.

If my experience making American folk toys is any indicator, you'll have a relaxing yet stimulating time cutting out, putting together, painting, and giving the toys in this book. When you've completed a toy, you can rest assured there's not another one anywhere exactly like it: You can even put your signature on it. And when you give a child a handmade toy with its roots in American history and folk culture, you link that child to the past as well as to yourself.

When a child sets one of these toys spinning, racing, dancing, tacking in a breeze, or sliding down a snowy hill, see if you come to my conclusion—that there is something unique about these designs: they carry forward, inexplicably, but certainly, soul.

A Cultural History of American Folk Toys

Two delightfully different 19th-century dolls capture the playful spirit of American folk toys. (Courtesy Pocumtuck Valley Memorial Association, Memorial Hall Museum, Deerfield, Massachusetts.)

The origins of nearly all American folk toys are shrouded in mystery. Where did our first cloth doll, spinning top, model sailboat, rocking horse, or board game come from? Who first gave names to the humorously designated "whimmydiddle" (also called a gee-haw), whirligig, or Ariadne's block? What farmer or wife, uncle or aunt first chiseled, whittled, knitted, or sewed any of dozens of different toys when this country was young? And when, where, and from what materials?

Attempts to answer such questions are little more than educated guesses since no written records exist. Yet it would seem logical that the colonists, who arrived in the New World with so little and must have so prized their children who survived—half the Plymouth Colony died in the first winter—would have been the first important toymakers. Nothing could be further from the truth.

The nearly complete absence of toys until 1750 in New England is a significant piece of our cultural history, because children's playthings were common in much of western Europe, particularly in Germany and France, and, to a lesser extent, in England. In fact, the recorded history of toys goes back to at least the ancient Sumerian cultures of the Middle East, where animal-shaped rattles were crafted for young children as early as 2600 B.C. We know that Egyptian and Greek dolls were fashioned before 2000 B.C., and the ancestor of the "Jacob's ladder" toy apparently turned up first in Tutankhamen's tomb, dating from 1352 B.C. Wheeled toys go back to at least 2000 B.C. Even Socrates mentions riding a rocking horse when he was a child! Something in early New England culture so clearly argued against children's play with toys, or any indoor play at all, that it is well worth investigating this striking dimension of our history.

A fanciful, painted terra-cotta image of a man riding on a goose. Greek, 5th century B.C. (Courtesy British Museum, London.)

Above: A handsomely carved and finished ivory toy dog in full flight, with an articulated lower jaw. Egyptian, 1570-1546 B.C.

Left: A marvelously stylized wheeled pull animal with two small pannier vases. Cypriot, c. 1200-1000 B.C. (Courtesy The Metropolitan Museum of Art, New York.)

The Puritan View of Childhood

The Puritans viewed children so differently from the way we do now that the terms "child" and "childhood" seem irrelevant in much of pre-Revolutionary American life. To the rigid Calvinist imagination, a newborn baby was a formless, inchoate lump of flesh, far more animal than human. Because of the newborn's reddish skin, curled-up body, and loud cry, many believed it a savage that could not be left to develop on its own. As the historian of childhood Glenn Davis points out, during this period "there was no image more popular than that of the physical molding of children, who were seen as soft wax, plaster, or clay to be beaten into shape."

It was the Puritan midwife who began to make the lump human. She placed the newborn on her lap just after birth and molded and kneaded the head, working out any bumps or asymmetrical parts resulting from the physical birth. She would then pull each arm and leg to its full extension, making the baby look temporarily "erect," and lastly focus her attention on the fontanel, the soft spot above the forehead. There she would work the skull bones toward each other, typically with her thumbs, and then, when the bones were as close as possible, she would bind up the head with narrow strips of cloth to hold the bones in position. For weeks after the birth, she would repeat the procedure until the fontanel was closed. It was widely believed that without this procedure, the baby would not achieve fully human shape.

The Puritans' vigilance at keeping the infant from reverting to its animal beginnings while hurrying it toward "adulthood" dominated many parts of early life. Above all, parents must keep the child straight in body, mind, and soul by voicing constant reminders. Joseph Cotton's catechism, written for young Puritans in the mid-17th century, taught children to repeat, "I was conceived in sin, and born in iniquity.... Adam's sin imputed to me and a corrupt nature dwells in me."

Cotton's grandson, Cotton Mather, by no means tempered his forefather's theology and preached to his flock: "Don't you know that your Children are the Children of Death, and the Children of Hell and the Children of Wrath by Nature?" No less an authority than Jonathan Edwards, dean of Calvinist divines, believed children possessed a natural tendency toward reversion and were in fact depraved, and that unrepentant children were "young vipers and infinitely more hateful than vipers."

To establish and maintain the child's "straightness," Puritans wrapped babies in swaddling, a three-piece equivalent of a straightjacket. First the legs were drawn out straight and bound, sometimes with cotton packing between the legs, from the ankles up to the chest. Then the arms were straightened and wrapped firmly to the baby's sides. Finally, a third piece of swaddling band wrapped the whole bundle. Thus were babies in New England kept warm and portable (like a loaf of bread!), but, above all, molded into the general shape of a straight-backed, straight-legged adult so that they would not crawl on all fours for the rest of their lives.

Boys and girls alike were prevented from crawling by dressing them in long petticoats, which made such four-limbed, animal-like locomotion impossible. When children were old enough to begin standing, they were hastened into a mock maturity by placing them in walking or standing stools. (Walking stools had wheels, while standing stools did not.) These short-legged stools had a large hole cut in the wooden seat where the child stood so the hole came to about the waist. Unlike the modern "walker," there was no cloth seat stretched between the stool's legs on which a baby could rest. Traditional wisdom held that crying was a natural exercise for the lungs, and infants and babies were not fully human anyway, so they were left in walking and standing stools for long periods to strengthen their legs.

Lois Orne by Joseph Badger, 1757. Young Puritan children were typically portrayed with solemn adult faces. Badger's tender study is one of the first American paintings to show a child with a toy. (Courtesy Worcester Art Museum, Worcester, Massachusetts.)

To accelerate the walking process, Puritan parents traditionally attached cords called "leading strings" around a toddler's chest and under the arms, and an adult holding the strings guided the early upright locomotion. Holding the child erect as though it were a puppet also prevented crawling. Young children were often hastened to this stage, and falls were common; to protect the head, parents placed a doughnut-like cloth tube stuffed with scraps of fabric around the baby's head. The protective doughnut, secured by a strap that went over the top of the head and tied beneath the chin, was termed a "pudding," and, as Mark Twain knew, a toddler wearing one was called a "puddin' head."

It was widely believed that infants who were bound and swaddled properly, had their limbs kneaded and pressed straight, slept in narrow, spine-straightening cradles, and were teased out of infancy with walking stools and leading strings would walk sooner and once upright become recognizably "human." And as human beings, they were insofar as possible considered miniature adults. Since Puritans discouraged play for adults, they discouraged it for children as well. Toys were considered frivolous and unproductive, and, most important, they distracted the young person from what was central in life—religion and work. Even dolls, a nearly universal toy worldwide over millennia, were suspect to the Puritan mind: Called "poppets," they could be the possessions of witches who used them in forbidden ceremonies and incantations.

Rather than leading the developing child toward exemplary behavior by example, the Puritans' operative word was often *correction,* or what we would call corporal punishment. The *New England Primer* taught the alphabet by little rhymes.

F The idle *Fool*
Is Whipt at school.
J *Job* feels the Rod
Yet blesses GOD.

And John Eliot, author of *The Harmony of the Gospels* (1678), gives the following advice to mothers: "The gentle rod of the mother is a very soft and gentle thing; it will break neither bone nore skin; yet by the blessing of God with it, and upon the wise application of it, it would break the bond that bindeth up corruption in the heart. ...*Withhold not correction from the child, for if thou beatest him with the rod he shall not die, thou shall beat him with the rod and deliver his soul from hell*" (italics mine). Parents were urged to use the whip or the rod to break self-assertion or "willfullness," and to substitute their own will for the child's.

No toys appear in paintings of American children before 1750. Clearly for the Puritan imagination, what we would call childhood did not really exist. At a time when childhood diseases were largely unchecked, infant mortality was high, and wives were expected to bear eight to a dozen children, there was little time to dote on the small, and the sooner they became adult, the better.

**"Prelude to Punishment,"
from *The Child and the
Republic* by Bernard Wishy,
1968. (Courtesy University
of Pennsylvania Press.)**

The Winds
of Change

So how did America move from this harsh, cruel, even brutal view of childhood to the child-centered world of today? The prime motivation was the political, social, and philosophical changes that swept through the 18th century. These changes, which led to anticolonialism, revolutions in America and France, and a vision of freedom broadly based on rationalism, profoundly affected the way people defined themselves, their aspirations, and their families and children.

The Bangwell Putt Doll, believed to be the oldest rag doll extant in America (c. 1765-1775). It is an exceptional piece of folk art, made with greatly oversized wooden hands for its owner, a young blind girl. (Courtesy Pocumtuck Valley Memorial Association, Memorial Hall Museum, Deerfield, Massachusetts.)

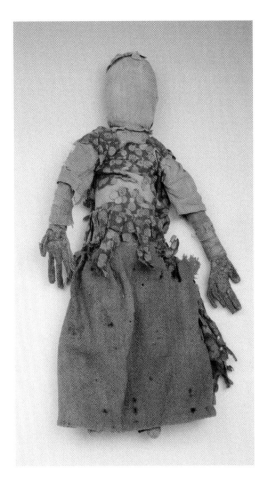

Once the Puritan definition of childhood was challenged by the new philosophy and science, it crumbled almost overnight.

By 1770, two remarkable transformations had taken place. First, all the paraphernalia of a Puritan infancy and early childhood had been tossed out: Swaddling, standing stools, walking stools, and leading strings were all consigned to the scrap heap. It was as though a pent-up wave had swept them away. Second, radically different ideas of what constituted a healthy child overwhelmed the old arguments, and with these ideas came a new definition of parental roles and the nature of childhood. John Locke, whose conceptions of freedom helped fuel the American Revolution and who had published *Some Thoughts Concerning Education* at the end of the 17th century, had his ideas rapidly appropriated by a nation amenable to change. There developed a new and serious interest in children themselves. The philosopher Jean-Jacques Rousseau wrote in 1762, "We know nothing of childhood. The wisest writers devote themselves to what a man ought to know, without asking what a child is capable of learning. They are always looking for the man in the child, without considering what he is before he becomes a man." One of Rousseau's chief ideas was to let children play, to allow them to experiment and improvise, and develop at their own speed.

Locke's and Rousseau's ideas were expanded by writers in England and America who sought to transform the upbringing of infants and children by demolishing the Puritan perception of the child as weak and uninteresting. These writers substituted the idea of childhood as a special and essential time when the young should be given greatly increased freedom to develop according to an inherent developmental progression. Locke was particularly influential because of his insistence that children *naturally* learn to crawl, then stand, and then walk if left alone. What children required most were intelligent limits to ensure their safety and guidance so that their naturally endowed talents and aptitude would blossom.

Crucial to this theory of development and education was *time*. Children needed time to develop their curiosity, motor skills, and sense of play and should not be rushed headlong into the society of grown-ups. This separate developmental stage became what we term "childhood," and, focused as it was

A beautiful rendering of Noah's Ark and animals, made in Germany and imported into the United States at the turn of the 19th century. (Photo by Richard Merrill; courtesy Peabody Essex Museum, Salem, Massachusetts.)

on natural progression, play, creativity, and curiosity, it followed that adults should supply children with safe and interesting objects to catch their fancies and stimulate their imaginations.

Something to Play With

From the late 18th century on, children of wealthy American parents had the toymaking factories of Europe at their disposal. They were typically given lead and tin soldiers and carved animals from Germany and Scandinavia, miniature English or Swiss sets of china for tea parties, and extraordinarily lifelike, wax- or porcelain-faced, ornately dressed dolls from England, Germany, and France. But what of the vast majority of the young population? For them it was up to the sewing and embroidery skills of their mothers, grandmothers, and aunts,

A highly wrought tin soldier of Frederick the Great (1775), by the famous German toymaker Johann Hilpert, who made 40 types of models of Frederick's soldiers. These toys became popular for young boys whose parents could afford to import them. (Courtesy the Germanisches National-museum, Nuremberg.)

Chloe, **an African-American rag doll, c. 1900. Her costume clearly identifies her as a domestic, probably in a wealthy family. (Courtesy Pocumtuck Valley Memorial Association, Memorial Hall Museum, Deerfield, Massachusetts.)**

Cornhusk doll made by the Penobscott Indians of Maine. These were some of the earliest dolls in Colonial America, given to young girls by friendly Native Americans. (Photo by Scott Phillips; from the author's collection.)

and the woodworking and metalworking skills of the men in the family.

The development of folk toys shares much with the evolution of folk painting and folk music. All three American forms of folk art began when someone wished to create something where previously there had been nothing—when a farmer or mechanic or quarryman or his wife or one of his sisters decided to fashion a cradle or a doll or paint a landscape on a wide-cut board or sing *a capella* about a family member or a wayward minister. Folk art takes the artistic materials at hand, does not wait for lessons, does not demand classical perfection, does not care what is hanging in the National Gallery, and strikes out boldly on its way.

Before the Civil War (1860-1865), the majority of Americans were farmers, who were familiar with basic tools. Many were immigrants who remembered European folk toys from their own childhoods. Greatly expanded world trade brought previously unseen toys from distant ports, including the yo-yo and the merry-go-round from China. The period from the close of the American Revolution until the Civil War became a golden age of American folk toys, a time when parents and relatives increasingly let young children play during part of the day for the sheer delight of it. To be sure, the greatest freedoms existed for the wealthy, and the misery of child labor remained all too common for the poor, but between these extremes the relatively new definitions of childhood made life significantly less constrained and fettered for large numbers of American children.

Few folk toys are wholly original. American folk toymakers were far more likely to work from someone else's toy, copy it out of accessible materials, improve it, give it another source of power, use a different color scheme with different paints or dyes, or fashion it with different proportions. They usually made the toy for themselves, for their own family, or at most in very small numbers. Commonly, toymakers worked in the home or, occasionally, in a small workshop (as contrasted with a factory), using simple hand tools and local materials, often scraps of cloth or wood and, less often, metal.

Most early toys were whittled or sawn by fathers and/or sewn by mothers. There were cornhusk, rag, and rope dolls, miniature cradles, hoop rollers, stilts, swings, and other simply constructed playthings. All were crafted by seat-of-the-pants engineering and common sense out of commonplace materials, but even more by an early

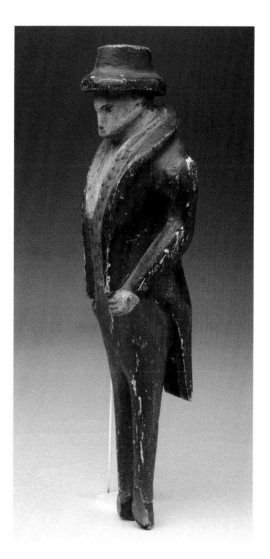

Hand-carved wooden female doll, c. 1810-1840. Her broken hat brim and feet show the probable effects of generations of play. (Photo by Amanda Merullo; courtesy Historic Deerfield, Inc.)

19th-century *Zeitgeist,* an Emersonian self-reliance that said something like this: Never see yourself as the have-not with your nose pressed against a window pane, enviously looking in upon what others own. Seize the materials and tools at hand and make it, fashion it, assemble it, dye the cloth in hot tea, color it with berry stain if that's what you've got, see it through, improve it, and it will soon be as good or better than what others have!

This was a fine opportunity for American ingenuity. You have no nails? Drill holes, carve thin tapered pegs, tap them into the holes, and then use your jackknife to slice the pegs off flush. No dowel? Find a straight tree branch. No wind-up spring? Use gravity, wind, or muscle power. No lathe? Rough out the wood with a saw, and then get to work with a jackknife, a file, and some patience. No hinges for a jack-in-the-box? Use small pieces of deerskin rubbed with fat until supple. No sized lumber? Take what wood you have, split it oversize, and handsaw and shave it to your needs with a jack plane. Most folk toys are made of fairly small pieces of wood, anyway.

From humble beginnings, when most children had access only to adult objects like ropes for jumping rope or tug-of-war or pots and pans to make noise and imitate mother, folk toys evolved into playthings that were specifically designed to encourage play and to provide a sense of delight. At first, a willow whistle or a spinning top was a prized possession.

Nineteenth-century American jack-in-the-box. The face is an excellent example of the demonic, whimsical, or bizarre in generations of this folk toy. (Courtesy New York Historical Society.)

Late 19th-century wooden spinning top. (Photo by Scott Phillips; from the author's collection.)

Late 19th-century self-propelled sled from Greenville, Maine. (Photo by Scott Phillips; from the author's collection.)

Simple, single-profile rocking horse made of hard pine with leather ears, date and place of origin unknown. (Photo by Stan Sherer; courtesy Hadley Farm Museum, Hadley, Massachusetts.)

A "shoofly" rocking horse for a young child, c. 1890. The horse is dapple gray, which was believed to be a lucky color. It has tongue-and-groove pine sides, with hardwood rockers and dowels. (Photo by Stan Sherer; courtesy Hadley Farm Museum, Hadley, Massachusetts.)

Then, with very few tools, a seesaw for good weather, an all-wood sled for winter, a simple kite for March breezes, a sturdy doll's cradle, or a rocking horse might appear.

Ethnic influences enlarged the available choices. The "Limberjack" (see p. 80) probably came through the Irish, for whom it provided rhythm in Celtic music (though its actual origin may have been through Sweden and central Europe). The "Carousel" (see p. 122) was probably Chinese but was rapidly modified to reflect American preferences in shape and color. Folk toys existed on a level where no patents or copyrights impeded the spread of copying, improvements, and fresh ideas.

As America moved toward the middle of the 19th century, more interesting and occasionally ingenious homemade toys increased in popularity, and a handful of toymakers began selling their wares. In 1850, the Bureau of the Census listed 47 toymakers, hardly a great number for a country of 23 million, but nevertheless significant because it shows how far conceptions of "child" and "play" had evolved in the previous 70 years.

By 1880, the Bureau of the Census reported 173 professional toymakers, and small factories mass-producing toys were springing up across the country. Many of them specialized in tin and cast-iron toys: This was the age of tin

Lever-powered tricycle, probably made by a small factory at the turn of the 20th century. Its wheels are wooden spoked, and the propulsion levers are lathe-turned hardwood; the front wheel is steered by the driver's feet. (Photo by Stan Sherer; courtesy Hadley Farm Museum, Hadley, Massachusetts.)

Horse-drawn Broadway taxi-wagon, a very sophisticated, spring-driven toy made by Stevens and Brown Co., of Cromwell, Connecticut, about 1860-1870, showing both originality and care in execution. (Courtesy Peabody Essex Museum, Salem, Massachusetts.)

vehicles, heavyweight mechanical banks, wheeled toys, and tin soldiers. By 1900, the United States had joined Germany and England as leaders in the global production of toys. But the small-scale or one-of-a-kind-for-my-daughter crafting of folk toys never stopped, and, especially in rural areas, it continues to this day.

Folk Toys Today

When you browse through an antique shop or a museum, there's little doubt that toys are among the most admired, provocative, and sentimental items in any period collection. Even if you've never played with a rocking horse, sled, dollhouse, or marble roller, these toys speak to the heart, memory, and imagination with great evocative power. They link us with our own beginnings, our love of play (perhaps much of it shared), and the delicate and wistful dreams of our own childhood. They link us, almost magically, to our larger cultural memories and our roots. It is little wonder that an antique dealer on Moosehead Lake, Maine, recently told me, "No, I hardly have a folk toy in the place; they are the one thing I can't keep in the shop. They just come in and go right out again."

But there is more than sentimentality at play here: Most folk toys are distinctly unlike what is presently mass-produced for children. My wife and I discovered that homemade toys (based on designs I had been collecting since 1972) had an immediate, powerful, and different appeal to our two children. To them, wooden and cloth toys were understandable. They demonstrated physical laws: the effects of gravity, inertia, rhythm, the fulcrum, or reciprocating movement. Some of the toys demanded patience. They provided exercise or required good eye-hand coordination. Perhaps most important, they supplied a sense of competence, or "can-do." Unlike a complicated and utterly inexplicable electronic plaything, in the unlikely event a folk toy broke, its structure was easily understood, and it was simple to fix. Folk toys are still with us and in use after all the bells and whistles of many contemporary designs have fallen silent. The strong, simple, homemade toy goes on, waiting to be picked up and played with. In this endurance there remains something important to human scale, something sturdy and reassuring.

Even though our two youngest children are now in their teens, they continue to be delighted when the seasonal toys they have known since infancy appear. Perhaps a small part of this pleasure resides in knowing that my wife and I made these toys for them when they were small. They regress happily. Everything I've learned about folk toys suggests that the same involvement, enchantment, and even love the boys have felt for these simple folk art forms will be passed on to their children as well.

The first folk toy collected by the author in 1974, a marble chaser built of resawn pine by Cliff Ashley, of Cushman, Massachusetts, from a basic pattern handed down by his grandfather. Mr. Ashley was 86 when he made this toy. Note where chutes have been broken and repaired because the author's children used the toy as a stepladder. (Photo by Scott Phillips; from the author's collection.)

Construction Materials and Tools

One of the best things about making folk toys is that you really don't have to spend a lot of money on materials and tools. Most of the toys in this book are fairly small, and none requires expensive materials or an elaborate shop. Early American toymakers would have used any wood that fit the bill and built most of their toys with the same simple tools they used for countless other tasks in their daily lives.

Hardwood, Softwood, and Plywood

You can make most folk toys from any kind of wood—including plywood—though some species have characteristics that lend themselves to toymaking better than others.

In any forest, hardwoods are easy to identify: They're the trees whose leaves turn glorious colors in the autumn. Maple is perhaps the most spectacular in hues and intensity, but cherry, ash,

beech, birch, and, to a lesser extent, oak (which likes to hold on to its brown leaves) fit in the same general classification. Softwoods, on the other hand, are evergreens, with needles instead of leaves; most lumber in the northern states is harvested from white pine, spruce, and fir. America has some great regional exceptions, though: Southern yellow pine is a gorgeous, very hard, and resistant pine, harder than some of the "hardwoods"; it was used in the last century for keels and skegs of sailboats. It is lovely for toymaking.

Hardwoods are tougher, usually a little heavier, and last longer in rough use than softwoods. The grain lies tighter together in hardwoods, making them stronger than the faster-growing softwoods. Hardwood generally stains more beautifully, or, like cherry, needs no stain at all. The rub is that hardwoods are not especially plentiful in lumberyards, they are more difficult to cut by hand, and they cost a good bit more than softwoods. Yet the cost-benefit equation favoring hardwoods makes sense: Most toys in this

American beech, commonly used for furniture and utensils, resists dents, finishes easily, and is a good choice for toys.

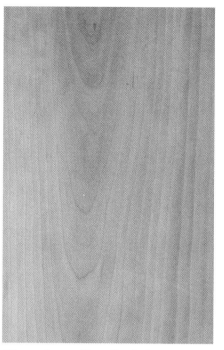

Cherry is excellent for lathe turning and takes a fine finish without stain.

Red oak, a very strong, open-grained hardwood, is plentiful and inexpensive and works well for toys subjected to rough use.

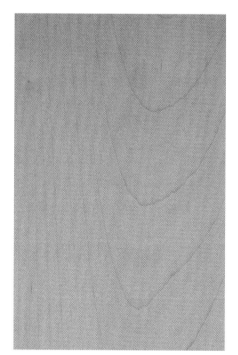

Red (soft) maple is close-grained and sands very smooth; it also takes stains well and paints easily.

Eastern white pine is plentiful, straight-grained, and easy to carve and saw but dents easily.

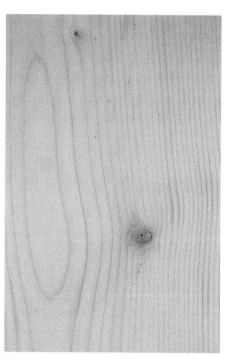

White spruce, common in framing lumber, varies in hardness but is usually fairly soft; it is a major source of 1½-in.-thick stock for toymaking.

book require so little material that the price differential is negligible. And hardwoods hold screws and other fasteners better, cut more smoothly, and resist dents and splitting. Furthermore, a sabersaw or scrollsaw cuts any hardwood with relative ease, and the increase in time to cut out a toy from maple or oak, when compared to pine, is negligible. So go with the best.

The same thinking should inform your choice of plywood. Use the highest quality you can find: It will resist water and splintering, have fewer "voids," and last longer than cheap plywood. If your plywood does have any small blemishes in the surface, they can be repaired with a fast-drying wood putty. One of the best buys for toymaking is shop-grade birch plywood. It has a very hard surface, stains well, sands to a smooth finish with little effort, and is strong. I used it for the dollhouse, the rocking horse, the checkerboard, and many small parts of toys in this book.

In a pinch, you can also use construction-grade plywood. The quality of each side of the plywood is graded: For example, "A-C" means that the "A" side is sanded and its imperfections have been cut out and plugged with a repair in the shape of a teardrop; the "C" side may have knots, some imperfections, and is unsanded. Much construction-grade plywood is made from fir and is very tough and resilient, and imperfections on the "C" side can be filled with wood putty. Most plywood now is glued with a urea-formaldehyde compound, and is thus highly water-resistant, but not truly waterproof.

CHOOSING THE RIGHT WOOD FOR THE TOY

When choosing wood for a toy, common sense is your best guide: Always use hardwood where the toy (or part of the toy) will receive rough use. For example, the self-propelled sled simply *must* have its handle and arms made of hardwood; you're asking for failure if you make them of a soft pine. Additionally, because sleds are left outdoors, they need the greater weather resistance of hardwood. Similarly, the spinning top should be turned of hardwood because just playing with it engenders rough use: spun at high speed, tossed in a toy box with larger toys, landing on the floor from table height and being stepped upon, it has a tough life. On the flip side, the carousel, an indoor toy that is gently wound up and let go, can be made successfully from softwood. The same goes for an

The cutoff box at a local lumberyard is a good source of scraps for toymaking.

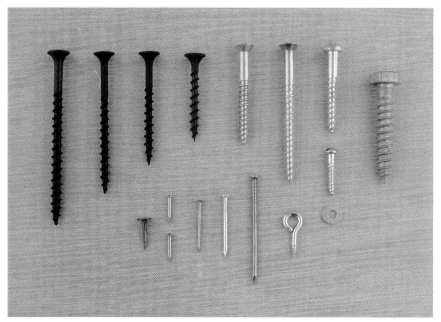

Typical fasteners used in toymaking include (top row from left) drywall screws, flat-head and round-head brass screws, a hex-head galvanized lag bolt, (bottom row from left) a blued steel carpet tack, brass escutcheon pins, steel headed brads, a finish nail, a small brass screw eye, and a brass washer.

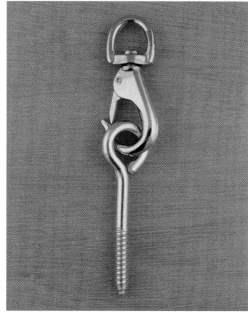

A threaded screw eye and swivel-base snap hook make the perfect fastener for rigging a detachable rope.

Bolts and nuts used in toymaking include (from left) two hex-head bolts and nuts, a carriage bolt and nut, and a round-head bolt with flat washer and nut.

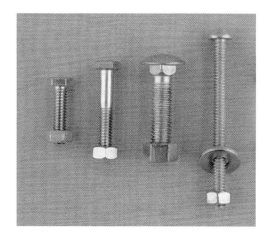

outdoor favorite, the sailboat, whose pine hull is large and strong enough to resist damage, and which needs to be light to achieve maximum buoyancy.

Plywood is an excellent choice where warping can be a problem, as, for example, on the rocking horse and dollhouse. For these toys, it's best to use shop-grade, not construction-grade, plywood.

Fasteners

Many of the toys in this book don't require fasteners; those that do use simple fasteners available at any hardware store. I favor using screws wherever possible, because they don't (or very rarely) come out, and that's a real plus around small children. Whenever possible, use screws and glue; you can use nails and glue, but rarely in toymaking do you want good-sized pieces held together by nails or brads alone.

Drywall screws are excellent for toymaking because they're easy to drive and require only a small (or no) pilot hole in softwood. They can usually be driven by a bit in a ⅜-in. drill, are cheap, and are available at any building-supply store. If you want to make your toys look more authentic, use regular slotted screws; I like to use round-head slotted brass screws with washers where they're visible because they dress up a piece of work and in small sizes cost little more than steel. Some larger toys require hex-head bolts, nuts, and flat washers.

Screw eyes commonly range from fasteners large enough to hold a two-person hammock down to those small enough for a thin string only. They have been an important part of toymaking for hundreds of years as the receiving end of catches, simple interlocking hinges, and anchor points for rope, cord, or twine.

Glues

Choosing a glue is like choosing your wood: Since you use so little, it makes sense to go with the best. Don't buy the inexpensive "white" glues commonly used for kids' projects. These glues are only moderately strong and are very vulnerable to moisture.

The glues to look for are those that call for overnight drying for maximum strength. My first choice would be a yellow-colored aliphatic resin "professional strength" or "professional quality" woodworker's glue; check to make sure it is water-resistant. When parts are likely to become very wet or submerged, use a slow-to-moderate-curing two-part epoxy. Epoxy is truly waterproof and tremendously strong but requires mixing, is more difficult to spread, and is more expensive than woodworker's glue. Use it on the sailboat and on any toy that spends part of its life outdoors.

Glues recommended for toymaking include (from left) water-resistant aliphatic resin wood glue, two-part waterproof epoxy, and an adhesive/sealant suitable for gluing cloth to wood.

How carefully you apply the glue will determine a lot about your finish. Excess glue that has squeezed out from a joint must be cleaned off, not smeared on the wood where it will inevitably attract fine sawdust and produce light spots in a varnish or stain finish. For easy cleanup, you can't beat aliphatic resins, which are water-soluble. But there is a hitch: The same water that makes cleanup easy can also seriously weaken the glue bond because it seeps into the joint, thinning the glue. To avoid this problem, remove all possible excess glue with a dry cloth or paper towel, and then get the last of it with a barely damp cloth. Never use a soaked sponge to clean up the joints. Another way to remove excess glue is to wait a quarter of an hour after clamping, or until the glue is just about set, and then remove the majority of it with a jackknife or chisel, ending with a final touch of a damp cloth.

Toymaking Tools

Most toys in this book can be cut out and assembled with simple hand tools; in fact, the designs of saws, hammers, brace and bit, hand drills, chisels, and the like have changed remarkably little since the early 19th century. It follows that you can experience a nice sort of historical connectedness with 200-year-old craftsmanship just by making these toys in the traditional way using hand tools alone.

Yet it is also true that, given the pace of modern life, many of us don't have the time (or realistically don't have the commitment) to turn out some of the more demanding toys with nothing but hand tools. Nor do most of us have the option of access to elaborate shops with every power tool imaginable to guarantee both speed and a high degree of accuracy. (Of course, if you have a table saw, bandsaw, scrollsaw, or lathe, there's no reason you shouldn't use them for toymaking.)

I have chosen a middle road in the no-power-vs.-power way of going about historical woodworking and provide instructions that assume you may wish to use two of the most common, flexible, and inexpensive power tools—a ⅜-in. electric drill and a sabersaw (also known as a jigsaw). These two hand-held tools speed up construction considerably.

HAND TOOLS

To make everything in this book except the spinning top and Tillie the Terpsichorean Queen, which require the high degree of roundness or trueness that only a lathe can provide, you can do just fine with hand tools and muscle power. Chances are that you already own or have access to several hand tools. Those you'll need are listed in the sidebar on the facing page and discussed below.

Measuring tools A carpenter's square (also known as an adjustable square) allows you to draw accurate 90° and 45° angles and is available with 12-in. and 16-in. rules. I recommend the longer rule because it in turn gives you a longer straightedge. Carpenter's squares are made with cast-iron or plastic bodies; an iron body keeps this versatile tool accurate much longer.

A compass is used to draw semicircles, arcs, and circles on wood or metal; choose one with a lock knob to keep the radius consistent as you swing the compass.

Measuring tapes come in all lengths and qualities; one that's 6 ft. long should suffice for toys, though a 25-ft. tape costs virtually the same amount. Use a moderately hard pencil that doesn't break on the uneven surface of most woods.

Useful measuring tools include a 16-in. carpenter's square, with cast-iron body and steel rule; a hard pencil; a retractable steel measuring tape with lock; and a compass with lock knob.

Cutting tools Coping saws are available with both wood-cutting and metal-cutting blades; for many small metal-cutting jobs they can take the place of a hacksaw. Choose a coping saw with the most robust frame available: You want to keep the blade, especially the metal-cutting one, under strong tension.

A crosscut saw is one of the most useful tools for toymaking. Choose one with a minimum of 11 teeth per inch to produce smooth cuts. Rip saws (8 to 9 teeth per inch) are no longer widely available in hardware stores and have largely been supplanted by the aggressive-toothed saw (see the sidebar on p. 28).

A backsaw is optional in your initial outlay, but it is a valuable fine-toothed saw that can be used in a homemade miter box (see p. 32) and as a crosscut saw on smaller pieces of wood. The stiff blade is easy to control.

THE TOYMAKER'S TOOLKIT

Almost all of the toys in this book can be built with hand tools. A few toys with turned parts (such as "Tillie" on pp. 140-143) require use of a lathe. The hand tools you'll need are as follows:

- carpenter's square
- compass
- measuring tape
- hard pencil
- coping saw
- fine crosscut saw
- rip saw (or aggressive-toothed saw, or pullsaw)
- rasps or forming tools
- chisels
- small or medium-sized plane
- jackknife
- utility knife
- straight-claw hammer
- hand drill and assorted bits
- brace, assorted bits, and countersink
- carpenter's awl
- four-tip screwdriver
- slip-joint and long-nosed pliers
- crescent wrench

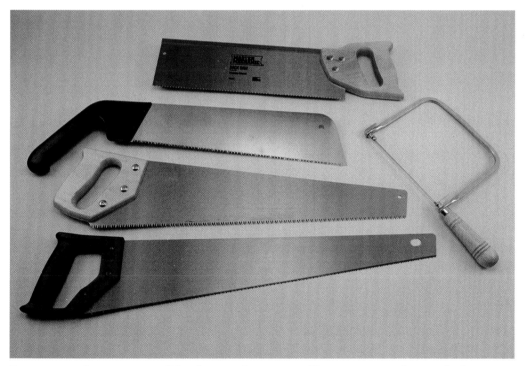

From top to bottom, a small backsaw, a Japanese pullsaw, an aggressive-toothed saw, and a fine-toothed crosscut saw. At right is a coping saw.

NEW DEVELOPMENTS IN HANDSAWS

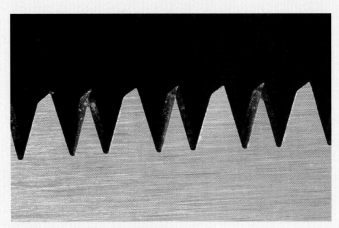

The teeth of an aggressive-toothed saw are cut deeply and alternate in long and short points.

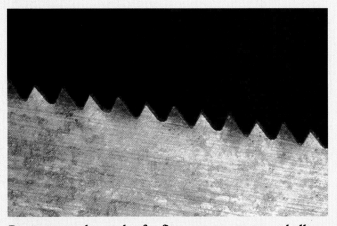

By contrast, the teeth of a fine crosscut saw are shallow cut and uniform, making for a very smooth cut.

Two fairly recent advances in American handsaw design are the introduction of the "aggressive-toothed" saw and the pullsaw. The aggressive-toothed saw, manufactured under several manufacturers' names, cuts faster than standard crosscut saws and features a different tooth design, where each tooth is sharpened on three faces and the run of teeth alternates long and short points. The saw both rips, cutting with the grain, and crosscuts, cutting across the grain; it cuts much faster than a traditional crosscut saw and about the same speed as a rip saw. One aggressive-toothed design can thus replace both standard rip and crosscut saws. So far so good. The only catch is that it makes a very rough cut as a crosscut saw, with a good deal of splintering, especially in pine. Even when you cut with a light touch, it splinters the wood significantly.

The pullsaw combines the aggressive-tooth configuration with a blade designed to pull rather than push. Japanese woodworkers have been using the pull design for well over 100 years, but it is new in American hardware stores. It has two great advantages: The blade does not bow or buck when you push it forward, and the backstroke, or cutting stroke, keeps the blade tight and straight all the way back. The main problem is that the workpiece must be secured very firmly to a bench or saw-horses because it wants to pull up with the backstroke. The workpiece can also vibrate, or "chatter," if you just hold it under your knee. The pullsaw cuts more rapidly than a standard crosscut saw and leaves a slightly smoother cut than the standard aggressive-toothed saw, but nowhere near as smooth as a 12- or 13-point standard handsaw.

Shaping tools Old-style cast-iron wood rasps have largely been replaced by lightweight, hardened-steel forming tools, with comfortable handles and (depending on the design) replaceable blades. One flat and one round forming tool are all you'll need.

When it comes to chisels, don't bother buying cheap ones—better to have one good ¾-in. chisel than four that won't hold an edge. The same applies for a small plane—a dull or poorly sharpened plane is worthless, but a classic low-angle plane with an accurate blade adjustment is one of the joys of woodworking, and it should last a lifetime.

Jackknives can be used for carving soft to medium wood; designs that prevent the blade from closing inadvertently are best. Because weight and grip are important, choose a medium to large jackknife for carving. I like a small jackknife for cleaning out half-set, excess glue. A utility knife with a cast-metal handle makes a surprisingly good instrument for carving, and replacement blades are inexpensive.

Fastening tools A hammer is one of the most basic of all hand tools; select one with a straight claw (which is much better than a curved claw for prying) and a good quality, straight-grained ash or hickory handle well wedged into the head.

Hand drills come in all sizes and prices, but for toymaking a small drill with a hard plastic handle and gearcase will suffice. Select medium-quality or better drill bits in ¹⁄₆₄-in. gradations. For drilling larger holes and countersinking screws, a brace and bit is the classic hand tool, but both the brace and bits have become rather expensive. Nevertheless, there is something undeniably passionate and satisfying about using the slow, quiet, human-powered brace and bit.

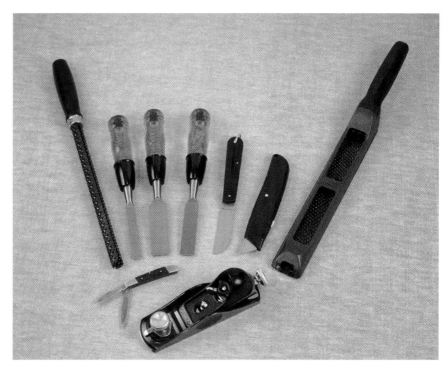

Handy shaping tools for toymaking include (clockwise from left) a round forming tool, three chisels, a single-blade carving jackknife, a utility knife with cast-iron handle, a flat forming tool, a low-angle plane, and a small jackknife.

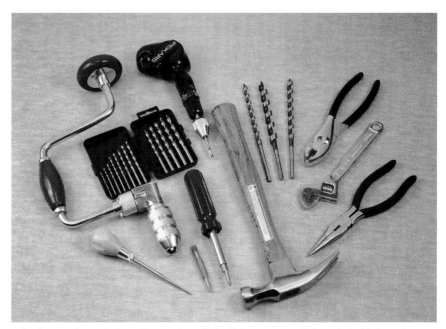

Clockwise from left, a brace, hand-drill bits, a small hand drill, bits for the brace, slip-joint pliers, an adjustable crescent wrench, long-nose pliers, a straight-claw hammer, a screwdriver with two Phillips and two straight-blade tips, and a carpenter's awl.

Good-quality used tools are easy to come by. The author acquired this collection at a local flea market.

A carpenter's awl is very useful for starting drill bits just where you want the hole, and a four-tip screwdriver (for medium and small Phillips and slotted screws) is the only screwdriver you'll need.

Two pairs of pliers, one slip-joint for general use and one long-nosed for close work, extend the power and dexterity of your fingers, and a medium-sized adjustable crescent wrench for holding and turning nuts and hex-head bolts completes your toolkit.

BUYING NEW OR USED?

The cost of new tools shouldn't stand in your way of acquiring good tools. One feature of contemporary American life is the large number of used hand tools available at very reasonable prices from garage sales and flea markets and through the want-ads.

Recently I visited several flea markets and garage sales that provided, along with plenty of junk, numerous high-

quality, low-priced, American-made hand tools with plenty of life left. For example, a Dunlap 16-oz. claw hammer cost $1; a Disston 13-point handsaw brought $2; an 8-in. Stanley plane, $4; a two-speed hand drill (patented in 1898) with ⅜-in. chuck, $12; a 19th-century Buck Brothers ⅜-in. chisel in new condition, $7; a Stanley 1-in. chisel, $3; and the seller threw in an old Buck Brothers gouge for nothing. The saw had some surface rust, but most came off with coarse steel wool and elbow grease. Professional sharpening for the saw was $7, for the plane blade $2, and for each chisel and the gouge, $1.50. Thus, the total outlay for a good hammer, a high-quality fine-toothed crosscut saw, an excellent plane, a reliable drill, two chisels, and a gouge was under $45. These used tools, which provide much of the hardware nucleus for a woodworking shop, cost under a third of store-bought tools (if not less), yet each works as well as new.

Sometimes garage sales provide breathtaking buys, as when a friend bought a fully equipped carpenter's toolbox with everything from hammers to backsaws, planes to gouges for $25. You never know what you're going to find. Generally, however, it's safer to buy used hand tools than used power tools, where hidden flaws (worn bearings, burned commutators) or poor previous maintenance may cause the tool, fully repaired, safe, and reliable, to cost as much as new, and you have no guarantee on the complete power tool. Flaws in hand tools (a cracked saw handle, a bent sawblade) are much easier to spot and to repair.

POWER DRILL AND SABERSAW

To save time and a certain amount of effort, you may wish to purchase two power tools—a ⅜-in., variable speed, reversing (VSR) electric drill and a sabersaw. Both tools are manufactured in a variety of styles, qualities, and prices, and have applications in home maintenance, wiring, plumbing, and construction of much larger projects than toys. Hardware stores, building-supply dealers, or discount houses with a power-tool department carry several brands of both tools.

Nearly any power drill or sabersaw will get you by, but my advice is to stay away from the bottom-of-the-line models, which are likely to burn out rapidly. Look for a power drill with ball bearings instead of sleeve bearings, a minimum 3.25-amp motor, and a design that balances well in your hand. Why ball bearings? Because they wear longer, stay lubricated for years, and usually double or triple the life of a power tool. Choose a sabersaw with a strong, well-made shoe (the metal plate the saw rests on) and ball-bearing construction. For a bit more money you can get a sabersaw with variable blade speeds.

Making Your Own Tools

Just as you can save money by buying used tools rather than new, you can also make some of your own tools. These include a small workbench, a miter box, and various files.

SMALL BENCH

It's hard to imagine making anything with tools without a sturdy bench to work on. You can of course use a woodworking workbench, but if you have only a small shop space, a good alternative is to build a sawhorse bench. The work surface is made from an inexpensive (imperfect or "second") solid-core door. These doors, which are typically 80 in. high by 32 in. to 36 in. wide and faced with birch veneer, can be cut down to fit your available space.

Support the door on two sawhorses, cut to about the same width as the door. Screw the door to the horses with four 3-in. drywall screws, countersunk ⅛ in.

A solid-core door and two sawhorses make a perfectly serviceable workbench for toymaking. The sawhorse on the right has a small, built-in tray to hold tools and supplies.

Use a carpenter's square to mark out the 45° angle on the miter box.

Cut the 45° miter with a crosscut saw, following the lines carefully.

into the door, to allow easy disassembly and storage. The sawhorses, constructed of 2x4s, 2x6s, and scraps of plywood and pine, nest on one another when stored to save space. The eight legs of the sawhorses give the bench real stability, and a small shelf on one of the horses provides tool accessibility.

MITER BOX

A simple miter box enables you to cut wood square and true and is quick and easy to build. You'll need two 14-in.-long pieces of ¾-in. plywood (one 4 in. wide, the other 3½ in. wide) and a 14-in.-long piece of 2x6 construction lumber trimmed down to 3⅝ in. wide. Assemble the ¾-in. plywood sides to the 2x6 base with 2-in. screws and glue. The 4-in.-wide side (the front) extends ½ in. below the base so that the miter box rests solidly against the edge of the bench. Mark out a 90° angle and a 45° angle with a carpenter's square, and then draw vertical guide lines to the base. Make the cuts with the same saw you'll do the mitering with.

BROAD FILES

Curved, and even straight, cuts from the saw are rarely perfect, so you'll need to do some smoothing before assembling or finishing the toy. You can buy files from any hardware store, but it's cheaper to make your own—and the tools are just as effective.

Broad files are made from cloth-backed belt-sander belts and rectangular pieces of wood (approximately 11 in. by 4 in.) that elongate the belt into a tough, double-sided sanding surface with rounded ends. I use 24-in. by 4-in. coarse and medium belts available from any hardware store.

You can remove a tremendous amount of wood quickly with the coarse grit, and

Coarse- and medium-grit broad files, four sizes of dowel files, and, at bottom, a common emery board for getting into tight spots.

the medium grit smooths things up nicely. The paper's surface does not fill up with sawdust but is open enough to keep coming back for more. The rounded end can be used to get into curves and reasonably tight places in your toy. When the end of the sanding belt starts to wear, advance it 2 in. or so to put fresh sanding material over the curve.

DOWEL FILES

Dowel files are inexpensive and easy to make, and help greatly to smooth out inside curves. Cut pieces 10 in. to 12 in. long from dowels of different diameters. Leave about 5 in. for a handle, and then cover the rest of the wood with various grits of sandpaper. Cut the sandpaper slightly oversize in width and glue down with a strong, flexible glue. With a sharp knife, cut the sandpaper to exact size once you've got it in place and the glue is beginning to set. Lastly, clamp down along the sand-

paper joint, covering the joint with wax paper before clamping.

One of the beauties of dowel files is their economy: You can make them from pencils, a piece of broomstick, anything that is round and long enough. The most useful grits are 100 and 150.

REINFORCED SANDPAPER

Sandpaper often rips long before it's worn out. One solution is to press nylon-filament-strengthened package tape onto the back of the sandpaper. It makes the paper last many times longer, especially when using a sanding block with sharp edges, which tend to tear ordinary paper.

Toymaking Techniques

Using a brace and bit, the traditional way to drill holes larger than ¼ in. diameter, is highly pleasurable and surprisingly quick.

For me, there's something undeniably grounded, elemental, and pleasurable in using hand tools. Who can resist the quiet, muscular enjoyment of a brace and bit, with the bit's fragrant cuttings multiplying around the deepening hole? Who doesn't enjoy the rhythmic sound of a crosscut saw, or the clean smell of shavings curling up from a sharp plane?

Folk toys do not require complex techniques—there is, for example, little or no joinery to cut—but it's important to master some basic techniques, such as cutting straight and curved lines and truing up cut surfaces. Making toys can be a way of learning hand-tool skills or a chance to rediscover skills long dormant. Whether you learn or relearn, you emerge ahead of your starting point, and end up with something to make a child smile.

Many "new" hand tools have barely changed since the 18th and 19th centuries. Working with a brace and bit, a hand drill, a wood-handled hammer, a saw, a plane, or an awl, you link yourself (without being self-conscious about it) to the history and craftsmanship of American folk art and folk toys.

Cutting a Straight Line

Cutting a straight line is the most basic of all woodworking operations. *Crosscutting* means cutting across the grain of the wood, while *ripping* describes cutting parallel to the grain.

CROSSCUTTING

Crosscutting is much easier than ripping because it cuts the wood fibers at an angle, slicing them off clean, rather than running among and between them with a tendency to skew away from hard spots in the wood, which is your saw's fate when ripping.

Now it's one thing to talk about a crisp, clean crosscut, and another to make one, but several choices can improve your results. First, select a saw with at least 10 teeth per inch, and preferably 12 or 13—a finer-point saw will push a lot more easily and save you a considerable amount of sanding. (Crosscut saws with 12 or 13 teeth per inch are not as plentiful as they once were, and you may have to look for one in a flea market.) Next, choose a saw with an accurate "set" to its teeth (where points are bent equally in an alternating left/right pattern). The blade can then clear out a gap (called a "kerf") slightly wider than the thickness of the blade, and thus prevent binding.

Also make sure that the blade is straight along its length. If it has a slight bow to one side, you can straighten the

Follow the line carefully when crosscutting a board to rough length.

blade by bending it by hand in the opposite direction and letting it spring back to its normal position. A straight blade doesn't vibrate but delivers all its energy (which you provide!) to the business of cutting.

To ensure an accurate crosscut, you need to draw a very legible line (and make sure you work in good lighting so you can see it). If you are squaring off the end of a piece of wood, say a 2x4 length of spruce, use a carpenter's square to draw a line at exactly 90° to the edge. Continue this line down the thickness of the board so you have two lines to guide

USING A MITER BOX

It's almost impossible for an amateur like me to make several perfectly square freehand cuts in a row. While the cuts may not look bad, my carpenter's square doesn't lie when I put it across the two planes of the cut.

The best way to ensure a square cut is to use a miter box, a simple tool that holds the sawblade square to the workpiece's width and thickness. (Directions for making the miter box are given on p. 32.)

The best saw to use with a miter box (especially in hardwood) is a backsaw, a fine-toothed crosscut saw with a rigid piece of metal, or "spine," about ¼ in. thick and ½ in. deep attached along the top of the saw. The spine prevents the blade from flexing while cutting. When cutting softwoods, however, a full-sized crosscut saw has enough blade stiffness to span the sides of the miter box, and it will give an excellent cut. A pullsaw also works well, although it must be used with light downward pressure on the blade, and the miter box must be screwed firmly to the bench (with the screws placed out of the blade's path). While fast, and smoother than a regular aggressive-toothed saw, the pullsaw is not as smooth as a standard crosscut saw with 10 to 13 teeth per inch.

When cutting 90° or 45° angles in the miter box, it's imperative that the workpiece not creep about as it's being cut. (And the harder the wood, the more likely that it *will* creep.) Use a clamp or two to hold it steady or screw the workpiece down to the box with two drywall screws.

Support the work in a home-made miter box to ensure a square cut. The saw shown here is a Japanese pullsaw.

the cut. If you follow the lines carefully, the workpiece will be true in length and the cut will be square to the surface. Another way to ensure that the cut is square is to use a miter box (see the sidebar at left).

Be aware of how you're holding the saw as you cut. Don't let it flop to one side or the other, but keep it running as vertical as you can hold it. After doing some crosscutting, you'll develop a feel for how the saw is running in the kerf; when it's perfectly vertical, it runs free and easy, with no binding left or right, and makes a nice even sound with lots of sawdust showering out with each stroke. A centuries-old trick a finish carpenter taught me is to keep the stub of a wax candle in your work apron or pocket, and rub it on each side of your saw's teeth after every half-dozen or so cuts. It's a bit like oiling a squeaky gate, and your saw will cut easier and faster, especially in hardwood.

Keep your saw razor sharp. To this end, when the saw is not in use keep the teeth covered with cardboard or a little sheath made of wood and held on with rubber bands; a saw just knocking around in a toolbox quickly gets dull. A sharp handsaw cuts farther along the line with each stroke, with less vertical swaying of the blade, and a diminished tendency of the blade to veer toward the softest wood in its path. (You want the saw to slice the wood's fibers cleanly, not bludgeon them to death.) I send my saws to a professional sharpening service when they get dull—you can tell when a saw is dull by the slightly rounded points on the teeth in the middle of the saw.

Handsawing is probably quicker than you think. With my sharp 13-point Disston flea-market handsaw, I can crosscut a piece of ¾-in. pine 4½ in. wide with about 15 strokes in 12 seconds; with the aggressive-toothed saw, 10 strokes in 8 seconds; and with the Japanese pullsaw, 6 strokes in 4 seconds. The big difference is in the smoothness of the cut. Speed has its drawbacks: The pullsaw and the aggressive-toothed saw leave a very rough cut in soft pine, whereas the old 13-point saw produces a nearly unsplintered surface. The two aggressive-toothed cuts can be made smoother by maintaining an artificially light touch downward with the saw, but then, of course, you sacrifice speed.

RIPPING

I've always found it harder to cut accurately with the grain than to crosscut, but if I pay close attention, I can make a decent rip cut. For best results, use a sharp 8- or 9-point ripsaw or an "aggressive-toothed" saw. Keep the sawblade at right angles to the work, taking long, smooth strokes with the teeth running about 45° to the surface of the board as you cut. Keep a close eye on the sawblade and the cut to make sure it is as near to 90° as possible.

The aggressive-toothed saw and the pullsaw do a much smoother job of cutting with the grain than against it. If you use a pullsaw, hold the workpiece down firmly with clamps or drywall screws, so that it doesn't lift upward as you make your cutting stroke. If you're new to ripping and are worried about ruining a good piece of wood, cut ¹⁄₁₆ in. outside the line (make sure you cut on the correct side of the line!). You can bring it down to exact size with a plane and broad file later on.

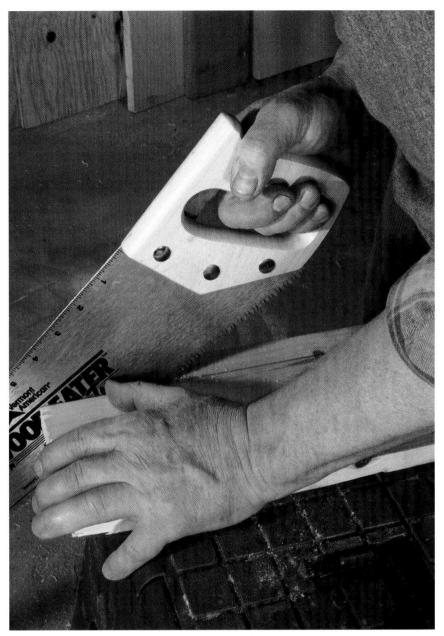

When ripping with an aggressive-toothed saw, hold the board down firmly and take long, smooth strokes with the saw at about 45° to the surface.

Use a coping saw to make curved cuts.

Cutting Curves and Circles

Just as it's more difficult to draw a perfectly even curve than a straight line, so is it more difficult to cut one. The problem is, of course, that your crosscut saw just won't curve around the line but wants to go straight, shooting off on its own. Here's where a coping saw comes in handy: Because it has a very narrow blade, this little saw allows you to cut around a curved line, while providing a reasonably smooth surface along the edge of the wood.

If you've never used a coping saw before, it can take a bit of getting used to. Here are a few words of advice: First, start with a sharp blade. Dull blades take forever to cut anything and are prone to bending, overheating, and breaking. Second, make sure the blade is under

adequate tension in the saw frame. If the blade bends too easily, even when the handle is screwed in tight, loosen the handle, remove the blade, and bend the frame ¼ in. larger. Then reinsert the blade, and tighten.

Third, take it slow. Because of their fine teeth and short stroke, coping saws take much longer to cut than rip or crosscut saws, so just enjoy the exercise, the sound, and the smell of the sawdust. Keep a sharp eye on the blade's angle to the wood—it should be at 90° to the wood's surface unless the plan indicates otherwise (and no plan in this book does). Also keep an eye on the line: It's easy to veer inside the line, especially if you're going too fast. When in doubt, pause. Cut a little outside the line, and true up with a broad file or dowel file. When you've finished a 2-ft.-long curved coping-saw cut in maple or oak, you can't help but feel a flash of real admiration for the 18th-century woodworker who produced brilliantly intricate and smooth cuts before the discovery of electricity and power equipment.

Cutting a circle is simply an extension of cutting a curve. Circular workpieces are easier to true up than complex curves, but only if the circle has a small center hole. Scribe the circle with a compass, mark the exact center with an awl, and drill an ⅛-in. hole through the center. Then, after the piece is roughed out with a coping saw, drive a ⅛-in.-diameter screw through the center hole, locating the workpiece on your sawhorse so that its circumference extends ⅛ in. or so past the end of the sawhorse. Then turn the workpiece by hand as you file the perimeter with a broad file. You can exert a great deal of wood-moving power downward from your shoulder, and quickly get the circle very close to true.

To get the circle closer to perfect, screw a small piece of wood onto the sawhorse about 1/16 in. outside the largest diameter of the workpiece. This piece of wood serves as a gauge. Rotate and sand the edge of the circle until the gauge is equidistant from all points on the perimeter.

Some of the toys presented in this book run on small wheels fitted to an axle. A hole saw is the ideal tool for cutting out the wheels (this suddenly dawned on me while I was drilling a hole with a hole saw: the "plug," the piece you normally throw away, is an almost perfectly round wheel with a 1/4-in. axle hole in its exact center). Hole saws attach to an arbor, which fits your drill's chuck, and follow a 1/4-in. pilot-hole bit that starts in the hole's center and keeps the hardened-tooth hole saw on course. Hole saws are manufactured in a variety of sizes, increasing in 1/8-in. or 1/4-in. gradations. Just remember that the dimension stamped on the outside of the saw is for the *hole* size, and that the plug (your wheel) will be about 1/16 in. smaller in diameter.

Hole saws come in two grades: soft-metal cutting and wood cutting. Metal-cutting hole saws cost about four times as much as those for woodcutting but keep a sharp edge when cutting many wheels in hardwood. Wood-cutting hole saws will keep an edge in softwood for several dozen wheels but dull fairly quickly when facing oak or ash. In any wood, keep the hole saw's teeth running cool by letting it spin free every five seconds or so.

If you want perfectly round wheels, you can use the hole saw to make blanks for turning on a lathe. Use a 2 1/4-in.-long by 1/4-in.-diameter bolt with two flat washers and a nut to hold the wheel in the lathe chuck. If you want, you can also make ornamental recesses or grooves in the wheel's side while you're turning and sanding to an exact roundness.

TRANSFERRING PATTERNS

Several of the toy projects in this book include patterns to help you reproduce curved edges and other nonrectilinear shapes. Transferring the outline of a toy from the page to a piece of wood is not difficult, but there are a few techniques that can make the process more accurate. You can transfer the image in three ways.

The most basic technique is to use tracing paper, which typically comes in 8 1/2-in. by 11-in. sheets. Simply place the tracing paper over the pattern and trace the toy's outline with a ballpoint pen; then turn the tracing paper over and scribble liberally on the back of the lines with a soft pencil. Tape the tracing paper to the wood, being sure to keep the wood's grain in the desired direction. Go over your traced line with a ballpoint pen, pressing down firmly.

The second technique is similar to the first, except that you insert a piece of blue or black carbon paper between the tracing paper and the wood when you go over the traced line (this eliminates the need to scribble on the back of the tracing paper after you've traced the initial outline). Using carbon paper can be a bit messy, but it produces a good legible line. Any smudges on the surface of the wood can be removed with sandpaper.

The third way to transfer a pattern is to use a photo-copy machine. This is the way to go when you need to scale up a pattern to full size. Use a high toner setting ("dark") when copying; then transfer the image to the wood using a very hot iron. It doesn't matter if you scorch the paper slightly.

The "plug" produced by a hole saw makes a perfect predrilled wheel for small toys.

Drilling

Using a hand drill or a brace and bit is fairly straightforward, but there are a few tips that can help you drill more accurate holes. First, always use a carpenter's awl to mark the starting point of the bit. This way, your drill bit won't wander all over the surface of the wood. Second, place a backing block under the workpiece to prevent splintered holes and torn wood fibers as the drill bit exits the hole.

Drilling holes at a perfect 90° to the surface can be difficult for beginners, so it's a good idea to set a small carpenter's square near the drill or brace and bit to serve as a guide. Sight along the vertical part of the square and align the drill bit with the edge of the square. Repeat this operation in two planes to get the bit perfectly upright forward and back and side to side. Once you get the hang of it (which shouldn't take long) you'll be able to dispense with the guide.

I'm particularly fond of the brace and bit and have to admit to using this tool in the same rather curious way my father did. He never turned a full revolution with the brace (except when starting the pilot screw) but always backed off with the ratchet after a semicircle of revolution, boring his way through in controlled, deliberate arcs of effort, the sharp metallic of the ratchet alternating with the cutting sound of the bit. It has occurred to me that perhaps his father made holes the same way.

Whittling

To cut small pieces of wood to almost any shape, try the ancient art of whittling with a sharp jackknife or a utility knife. Make small cuts, always moving the knife away from your body to avoid injury. The harder the wood, the smaller or shallower the cut; remember that a sharp knife is safer than a dull one. When whittling a symmetrical shape like a boat hull or a doll's head, compare the two sides often, and where possible, fit your work to a template.

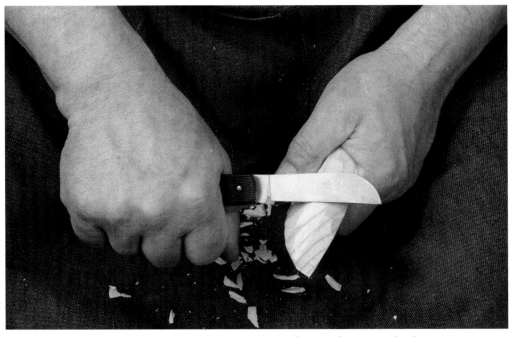

When whittling a piece of wood, always move the knife away from your body.

When truing up a cut surface with a plane, butt the end of the workpiece into a stop fastened to the bench.

Truing Up the Workpiece

To ensure strength and a good fit, always true up cut surfaces before gluing (and always "dry-fit" all pieces before final assembly). A plane is the perfect tool for smoothing a rip cut.

To plane a ripped edge, first screw a small U-shaped stop or "keeper" on your bench (see the photo above). Where possible, try to plane in the same direction in which the grain rises in front of the plane so that the blade does not dig into the wood by following the downward grain marking. Set the plane to cut very thin shavings, put the end of the workpiece in the stop, and shave the wood down to the line. Planing is one of those rare exercises where less is definitely more—where cutting a thin shaving of wood works far better than tearing out a thick one—in making your joint perfectly smooth, especially in hardwood.

Use a coarse broad file to smooth wood to a line on a cross-grain cut.

Broad files are ideal for truing up cross-grained edges. I find it best to start with a coarse 50-grit file, and then move to a 100- or 120-grit paper. Broad files are used not only to true up cut surfaces before gluing but also to prepare the toy for finishing, the subject of the next chapter.

Finishing

The toy parts are cut out, one subassembly is glued and screwed together, and now the glue has set. You step back and take a good look at what you've made: In all honesty, it seems a far cry from the endearing piece of folk art you had in your mind's eye. Some of the cuts are ragged, the wood itself is rough in places, and a hammer blow has left a dent in a noticeable spot. While the basic design is pleasing and the construction is strong, the whole thing looks, well...crude.

Fear not! Your project is just about par for the course. Broad files and sandpaper are two of your best friends in cleaning up your work, and with a little time and attention they can make a huge difference in the appearance of the toy. What's more, many of the toys presented in this book are finished with paint, which can cover a multitude of sins. Regardless of whether you intend to finish your toy, here are a few suggestions for cleaning up its appearance:

• If a cut is well outside a line, say ⅛ in., use a 50- or 60-grit broad file to get close, and then sneak up on the line with 120 grit. Wherever possible, sand with the grain.

• If you've cut slightly inside a line, fair the cut with a broad file until it conforms broadly to the rest of the design. No one except you will notice a small variation in symmetry. Sometimes you can make the toy's opposite side conform exactly to the new faired line with no appreciable loss in appearance.

• Use a dowel file to remove sawcut marks from inside curves. Always use the largest diameter of dowel file that fits.

• Use an emery board (made for fingernails) to sand in tight places. Most boards have medium and fine grits on opposite sides.

- If the surface of the wood has a small dent, pour some boiling water on the dented surface and let the wood dry overnight. If boiling water doesn't swell out the dented wood fibers enough, sand the whole surrounding surface until the dent disappears. Most toys tolerate small variations in thickness. Alternatively, just live with the dent—folk toys don't have to be perfect.

- Fill any deep dents, voids, or gaps with fast-drying wood putty. Sand off all excess and, if necessary, apply a second coat.

- Sand a small curve or "radius" on all edges. It will help even out small variations in the toy's outline, make the edges less likely to split, and also help any paint or varnish stay on the toy.

Preparation for Finishing

A good finish not only makes your work more appealing but also helps to protect the wood and create a more durable toy. Whether you use paint, stain, or varnish, the key to a good finish lies in the surface preparation.

SANDING

While coarse-grit sanding belts are ideal for making broad files to true up ragged cuts, you'll need flat sheets of finer aluminum-oxide sandpaper for preparing the surface for a finish. I use two grits of sandpaper for finishing—150 grit (fine) and 220 grit (extra fine)—both purchased in full-size sheets (9 in. by 11 in.). The 150-grit paper removes small surface irregularities and cleans the wood, while the 220 grit leaves a super-smooth finish.

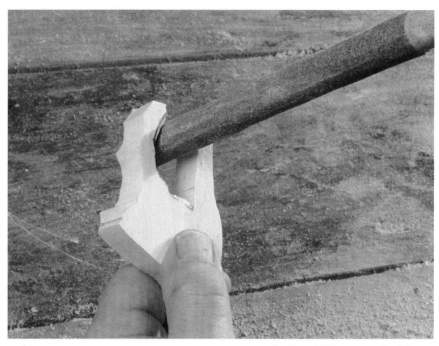

A dowel file covered with medium-grit sandpaper comes in handy for cleaning up a ragged cut in a tight spot.

Pine and other softwoods sand very quickly but also scratch easily, so you need to pay close attention to your technique, sanding with the grain and using a light touch to finish off. Don't sand across the grain or you'll leave noticeable scratches. Hardwoods take more time to sand but often have fewer dents or imperfections to begin with by virtue of their hardness.

One of the best ways to keep your sanding even and also to preserve the sandpaper is to make a sanding block. I make blocks from scraps of pine sized to hold a quarter sheet of sandpaper. A 3-in. by 5½-in. pine block ¾ in. thick will give you ¾ in. of sandpaper to fold and tack down on the long sides of the block. Round over the sides of the block slightly so that the paper doesn't tear. Attach the sandpaper tightly with three thumbtacks on each long side. For more aggressive sanding, make your block from a scrap of 2x4 construction lumber, which is actually 3½ in. wide by 1½ in. thick, cut the same 5½ in. long. It's a little more comfortable to hold and bear down on, but not quite as maneuverable.

Painting

For the most part, painted toys are a lot more fun for children to play with, kindling the imagination with their color and detail. By their very nature, most toys in this book look better painted than plain—just picture the rolling acrobat shown below without paint and you'll appreciate what I mean. But paint is more than just a pretty face. It also forms a barrier film on the wood's surface that keeps out moisture and protects the whole toy. Painted toys invariably last longer than unpainted toys.

CHOOSING A PAINT

There are several things to consider when choosing a paint for toys. First and foremost, it must be safe; always check the label to make sure the paint is nontoxic. The paint must come in strong, bright colors; it must mix smoothly and easily; it must adhere well to the wood; it must cover well; it must produce a good finish; and it must be easy to clean up. In my experience, the hands-down winner on all counts is water-soluble acrylic enamel. Hobby, craft, and some hardware and discount stores carry several brands of these new paints: For the toys in this book, I used colored enamels by Delta Ceramcoat and Accent Acrylic. They are both color-fast, easy to apply, and very simple to clean up.

One of the unexpected pleasures of using acrylic paints is that they're so easy to mix to create your own special colors. Each comes in a small squeeze bottle (2 oz. or 8 oz.) with a $\frac{1}{16}$-in. hole in the cap; the contents can be counted out drop by drop and recorded on paper to preserve a "recipe" of a particular pink, vibrant orange, or lime green. I use ordinary screw-type, one- or two-liter bottle caps for mixing small amounts of paint and small jar tops for larger amounts.

If you plan to make several of the larger toys, it may make sense to buy quarts of acrylic paint. Most hardware

Painting a toy in bright, vibrant colors can really add to its appeal.

A toymaker's paint shop set up on a card table covered with newspaper. The bottlecaps provide ideal containers for mixing small amounts of paint.

and all paint stores will custom-mix colors for you in larger volumes for half the price of craft-shop paint. Many paint stores now also have color-matching computers. If you want to match an antique or highly unusual color (say, from a piece of cloth or a family heirloom) and can get a sample of that color to the paint store, a color scanner will look at the sample and tell you the exact formula for the additives to make a match.

Finally, a word on spray paints. Many toymakers like the quickness and convenience of spray paints, which put paint on a surface as quickly as you can push a button. But they have two significant drawbacks. First, you can't mix colors to get the shade and intensity you want, and, second, spray-can paints

produce a different finish texture from that found on traditional folk art of all kinds. Brushstrokes in the paint's surface characterize folk toys back to their very beginnings.

BRUSHES

You'll want about four brushes for the variety of toys in this book. A 1½-in. brush for acrylic latex (as fine-bristled a polyester or nylon as you can find) works well for the large toys, like the sled and the rocking horse. A ⅝-in., squared-off artist's brush is fine for overall painting of smaller toys. To cut in the color, a ¼-in. round brush does the job nicely, and for fine work, like painting in animals' or dolls' eyes, use a ⅛-in. round brush that comes to a good point.

Small brushes are like most everything else: You get what you pay for. Genuine sable-hair brushes—whether tapered square-ended or round shaped to a perfect point—allow any paint, whether oil or acrylic, to flow beautifully; these are the brushes that professional artists paint with. If money is no object, you can use them too. Art-supply stores and craft shops also carry moderately priced good-quality nylon or polyester brushes for about $2 to $4 each, and these will do very well for toymaking. If money definitely *is* an object, you can make usable pointed brushes for acrylic paint out of your kids' very inexpensive watercolor brushes by tapering them to a point using fingernail scissors.

If you want to reuse your brushes, it's important to clean them once you're done painting. One of the joys of using acrylic paints is that they're so easy to clean up. I fill three small cans with warm water and work each brush in each in turn. When the brush comes

from the last can, it is really free of color. A scrap of bath towel works well to absorb the thinned-out color from the bristles.

DO YOU NEED TO PRIME?

Some people favor applying a coat or two of clear shellac or varnish undercoat before you paint with color to get smoother, more professional results while using less colored paint. Although this procedure may work well for boat or car models that are intended only for display, I don't recommend it for hands-on toys because the acrylic paint doesn't adhere as well to varnish and shellac as it does to bare wood. Whenever I've tried varnish or shellac primers, the acrylic paint has tended to chip off in the rough and tumble world of children's play.

You can of course use an acrylic primer, one that is specially formulated for acrylic paint for wood surfaces. It will save you a coat of color paint, but from my experience it doesn't really improve adhesion.

APPLYING THE PAINT

Acrylic paints are easy to apply, but there are one or two things to watch out for. First and foremost, don't overload the brush—dip the bristles only about halfway into the paint. Take long, even strokes on large surfaces and, if necessary, add a drop or two of water to the mix to keep the paint flowing smoothly. Where two colors meet, creep up toward the line slowly—don't go in with a full brush or you won't be able to cut an accurate line. (For more tips on cutting in lines and curves, see the sidebar on the facing page.)

Toymaker's brushes include (from left to right) a 1½-in. brush for large projects, an ⅛-in. round brush with a sharp point for detail work, a ¼-in. round brush to cut in color, and a ⅝-in. squared-off artist's brush for painting small toys.

MASKING TAPE:
THE TOYMAKER'S BEST FRIEND

Some of us have steady hands for painting and love to cut in complex curves. Others have neither the steadiness nor the love and dread the thought of trying to paint a curvilinear line of, say, red against white. For these souls, my advice is to let masking tape make it easy.

Masking tape can be a little tricky to get the hang of at first, so here are some helpful pointers. First, always use fresh tape. Old or dried-out tape will tear off unevenly, and the glue will be unequally spread on the back side. Use narrow tape—½ in. is plenty wide enough. Paint the lighter color first, and let it dry overnight (at this stage, it doesn't matter if it goes over the line slightly). Then put masking tape along the line of demarcation, pressing down the tape with your fingertip until it's firmly adhered along the edge that separates the two colors. Build up two or three coats of darker color, and then remove the tape while the paint is still tacky. Don't leave the tape on for too long because it can pull up the paint when you remove it.

Straight edges are easy to mask off, but what about curves too sharp to follow with the edge of ½-in. tape? No problem—as long as you use extra-narrow tape. Using a single-edged razor blade or a utility knife, make two careful cuts into the face of the masking tape, ⅛ in. from each edge all the way around the roll. Each layer of tape on a standard roll is about 12 in. when dispensed out, so you don't have to make too deep a cut to get 24 in. of ⅛-in.-wide tape. This narrow tape will follow much more serpentine curves than the ½-in.-wide tape yet still give you a lot of help in painting a clean line. When you pull the tape off the roll, you'll get two "factory edges"

(outside edges) of ⅛-in.-wide tape per length of the ½-in. masking tape. Stick the narrow tape down carefully, following the instructions in the previous paragraph. Paint the color you want, and then remove the tape. The line between colors should be crisp and accurate.

Don't worry if there's a small glitch—a small burble of color that has seeped under the tape. If you want, you can touch it up freehand, or you can just let it go. Just remember, folk toys don't have to be perfect.

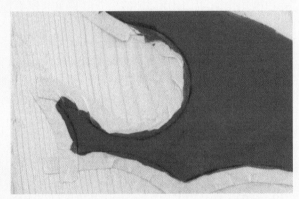

Narrow, ⅛-in.-wide masking tape is ideal for demarking a sharp curve.

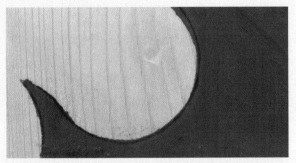

With the tape removed, the line is clean and accurate.

Your first coat of paint (or shellac or varnish) will make tiny pieces of the wood's grain stand up, like peach fuzz, so that the wood is often rougher after a first coat than it was with no paint. And because the cellular structure of all wood, especially softwood, is uneven, some areas will absorb the initial paint more than others. A light sanding with 220-grit paper will even out the first coat as well as cut off the fuzz at the paint level.

Don't be upset if you sand off most of the first coat of color! Even though paint doesn't sink deep into the wood, your initial coat will have filled the pores more than you think. As long as the wood is clean and free from nonsticking materials like oil or soap residue, the acrylic finish will adhere well.

You'll find that softwoods usually take three coats of colored paint to make the color uniform and show its full intensity. After the second coat has dried, you can determine by touch whether it needs another sanding with 220 grit before the final coat. Hardwood usually requires only two coats of paint.

Staining

Most toys take well to bright colors, but some, like the climbing bear, look just as good natural or stained. For example, if you make the little climbing bear out of a hardwood like cherry, there's really no need for stain—it's hard to improve on the lovely, dark-reddish-brown color of the wood with a simple oil finish. But unfinished white pine tends to show dirt, and darkening it is simple with a stain.

Begin with careful surface preparation. Stains show scratches and imper-

fections in the wood far more than paints, so at the very outset choose a particularly clear piece of wood. Then sand the edges more carefully than you would for paint. Use 150- and 220-grit sandpaper liberally to get the sawcut marks to a minimum and continue with both grits over the whole surface.

CHOOSING A STAIN

There are two basic types of stains: pigmented and dye colored. Both are available in water-based and oil-based forms. For toymaking, I use pigmented stains exclusively because they help show off the grain of the wood. The majority of these are oil based. Pigmented, oil-based stains often require serious mixing, so remove the cover from the can of stain, loosen up the pigment on the bottom with a stirring stick, and keep stirring until all the pigment is dissolved. This operation may take 10 minutes if the stain has been sitting for several months.

APPLYING THE STAIN

Test the stain on a scrap of the same type of wood you're staining to see how you like the color. Pigmented stains penetrate the wood rapidly, so you'll have a good idea within a minute or two of how the color will look. Apply the stain with a sponge brush or a small piece of cotton cloth, and then wipe down with a dry cloth two to three minutes later. Wiping the stain will generally lighten the color and remove any lap marks from the application. A second or third coat of stain will darken the color, but only slightly.

If you want to varnish the stained toy, use a varnish that's compatible with the stain. If you've used an oil-based stain, use an oil-based varnish such as

A variety of finishes on sanded spruce: (from left to right) a light stain, one heavy coat of three contrasting colors, and a water-based varnish.

a marine or polyurethane type. A water-soluble stain should be followed by a water-based varnish. It's often a good idea to use stains and varnishes produced by the same company. If you want to save a step, there are a limited number of stains available already mixed with varnishes.

Varnishing

My favorite varnishes are the standard, old-fashioned, oil-based types, which are very simple to apply and lay down a tough, protective coat. "Marine" or "spar" varnish comes in gloss and flat finishes, and stands up extremely well when a toy gets wet. Satin finishes of all varnishes are fine but generally not quite as tough as gloss, so you may want to apply an extra coat. Several companies make an amber-colored varnish, which imparts a slightly antique appearance to a toy.

A second type of varnish is oil-based polyurethane, which is known for toughness and is now used almost universally for wood-floor finishing. Polyurethane works well for indoor toys but does not stand up as well as marine varnish to outdoor extremes of heat and cold, which expand and contract the wood.

The latest varnishes to hit the market are the water-based urethanes. While these are the easiest to apply and clean up (just add water), for me they have been the least successful. They don't darken the wood, making it look "varnished" (an aesthetic objection), and don't seem to resist water and stand up to rough use as well as the oil-based types. One brand I tested blushed white whenever the varnish got wet.

Projects

Whimmydiddle

The whimmydiddle is not only one of America's stranger-looking folk toys, but it also has one of its weirdest names. Its roots go in at least two directions: Native American children played with whimmydiddles, calling them hoo-doos, and European sorcerers in the Middle Ages used them to cast spells and to detect lies.

Its roots and name aside, the whimmydiddle's chief claim to fame is the mysterious movement of its propeller, which has endeared it to generations of children, and some young in heart only. It's hard to explain why rubbing back and forth along the "vertebrae" of the whimmydiddle makes the propeller spin like crazy, but, take it from me, it does. And different methods of rubbing the whimmydiddle can make it spin clockwise or counterclockwise, or even stand still. (The secret is to rotate the "body" slightly left or right while you zip the rubbing stick back and forth across the notches.)

Because the propeller will rotate to the right or to the left, the whimmydiddle is also called a "gee haw," a shout given to a work horse to make it turn right or left. There's even a poem about this bizarre little toy:

"It's the physical, gee-whizmical
*   mysterious invention,*
It's a chemical, gee-whimical delirious
*   convention,*
It's a go left, go right, stop in the
*   middle,*
It's a gee whimmy, haw whimmy,
*   gee haw whimmydiddle."*

The Annual Gee Haw Whimmydiddle Convention is held in August in Asheville, North Carolina, with entrants zipping their whimmydiddles with all manner of fancy moves. The prize? You guessed it: a gold-plated whimmydiddle.

The Appalachian whimmydiddle is typically carved from laurel or rhododendron wood and, unlike the straight, dowel-based model shown here, has a short fork in the wood. The fork acts as a handle, with the notches being carved in the longer part of the Y.

How to Make the Toy

Nothing about the whimmydiddle is according to Hoyle. You may want to customize one for a child, making the handle a little longer or shorter to fit the child's hand. There's only one thing that's really important—the propeller must balance perfectly to get real speed out of this strange beast.

1 Cut nine V-notches in the longer dowel. The notches should go about halfway through the diameter of the wood.

2 Round over the end of the dowel handle. Taper the opposite end (the propeller end) to a gentle, blunt point.

- **dowel or section of tree branch about 10 in. long, nominal ⅜ in. dia. (body)**
- **dowel or section of tree branch about 6 in. long, nominal ¼ in. dia. (rubbing stick)**
- **⅛-in.-dia. dowel, 1¼ in. long (propeller)**
- **small headed brad, ⅜ in. to ⅝ in. long**

WHIMMYDIDDLE

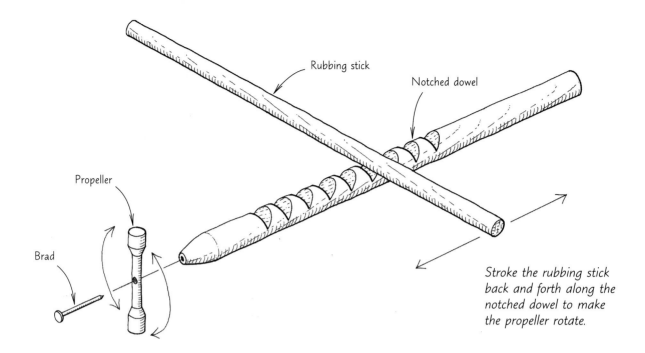

Rubbing stick

Notched dowel

Propeller

Brad

Stroke the rubbing stick back and forth along the notched dowel to make the propeller rotate.

3 Shape the propeller out of ⅛-in.-diameter dowel. Measure to the midpoint of the dowel and drill a ¹⁄₁₆-in.-diameter hole. Whittle and sand to a dumbbell shape. Insert a small headed brad into the hole and balance the propeller, gently sanding wood off the heavy end.

4 Drill a hole in the end of the dowel body. If you don't have a drill bit the size of your brad, cut the head off the brad and use it in your drill. After boring the original hole, take the brad out, and using a hammer, tap the pointed end on a hard flat surface to turn the end into a slightly larger diameter. Then re-bore the hole, and the propeller should spin nicely.

You can make whimmydiddles in the workshop, but they're also great toys to make when you're out walking or camping in the woods. All you need is a jackknife with a sharp point and a small-diameter headed brad. Make the whimmydiddle out of whatever small branch is at hand, and the propeller from a bit of twig. Bore the hole in the propeller with your jackknife, and then tap the brad into the whimmydiddle with a rock.

Climbing Bear

- 1 piece 7-in. x 6-in. x ¾-in. hard pine (bear)

- 1 piece 7¼-in. x ¾-in. x 5/16-in. hardwood (toggle bar)

- 3-in. length of 7/16-in.-dia. dowel (keepers)

- 9-ft. length of 3/16-in.-dia. nylon cord (48 in. for each pulling cord, 12 in. for the toggle hook)

If you want to make a quick and easy toy for a small child, the climbing bear is a sure winner. It takes less than an hour to complete, and has been a folk-toy favorite for generations. Exactly why the bear climbs is something of a mystery, a fact that makes children appreciate it all the more.

To send the bear up the cords, hang the loop of the toggle bar from a nail or hook at a height from the floor that leaves the bear dangling at a level easily reached by the child. Then pull down on one little handle, then the other, and alternate until the bear reaches the top. (You can also pull both handles apart to make the bear scoot up the cords pronto.) Let go of both sides to send the bear swooshing back down to the bottom.

How to Make the Toy

1 Use a photocopy machine to scale up the pattern of the bear to full size. Place the copy face down on a piece of ¾-in. hard pine (or hardwood) and use a very hot iron to transfer the outline to the wood. Spend time especially on the bear's eyes, nose, and mouth.

2 Cut out the bear with a coping saw or sabersaw, and then true up any rough

CLIMBING BEAR

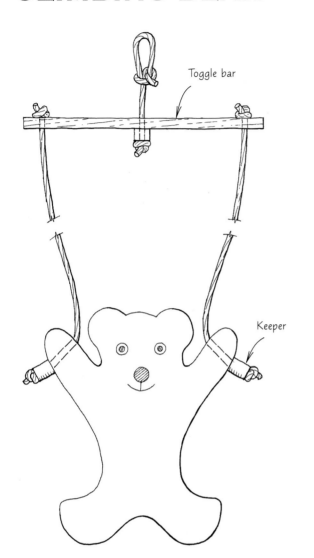

Toggle bar

Keeper

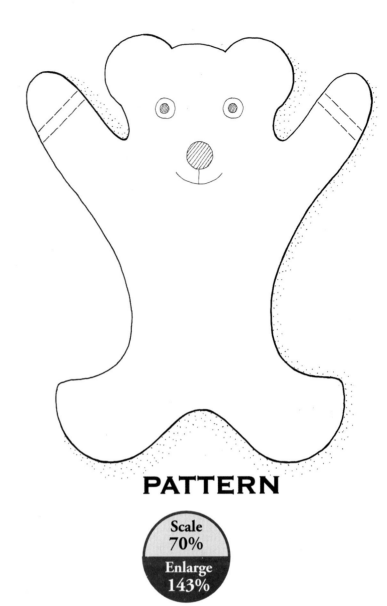

PATTERN

Scale
70%

Enlarge
143%

edges with broad files and dowel files. Carefully drill holes for the cords in the bear's arms. As you may have guessed, the angle of the holes is critical to making this bear keep on climbing. A 45° angle seems to work best.

3 Cut out the toggle bar from ⁵⁄₁₆-in.-thick hardwood and drill three holes as shown in the drawing above.

4 Cut three "keepers" from the ⁷⁄₁₆-in. dowel and drill a ³⁄₁₆-in.-diameter hole in each.

5 Thread two lengths of nylon cord through the keepers, the bear, and the toggle bar. Use a short length of cord for the toggle hanger, forming the cord into a loop. Secure the keepers with overhand knots and use a soldering iron to melt the knots slightly so they won't come apart under hard play.

6 Touch up the detail of the bear's face (front and back) with magic marker or pencil.

7 Stain the bear with a medium tint, or if time is short, just hand the toy over smelling of fresh pine.

Color Wheel

I got the idea for this toy from the color wheels my mother used to make for me and my two brothers during World War II, when money for toys was hard to come by. She would take a round cardboard top from an old-fashioned glass milk bottle and color it with wax crayons—red and yellow on one side, blue and yellow on the other. Then she'd thread a big needle with carpet thread, pass it through the milk-bottle cap twice, and knot the thread into a long loop. With the loop wrapped around her hands, she'd set the cap spinning, and before you knew it, the red and yellow turned orange and blue and yellow became green in a blur of gently whirring magic.

You can, of course, still make im-promptu color wheels from a cardboard disc or a button and thread, but they usually don't last very long. I made the model shown here of plywood, which is almost indestructible, and used mason's line, a very tough type of string. Another advantage of using plywood and making the wheels large in diameter is that they spin at quite a clip.

To wind up a disc, hold your hands a little under 2 ft. apart, with the string moderately loose, and begin a circular motion of both wrists in the same direction (it doesn't matter if you wind toward you or away from you). When you've got about 20 to 25 twists in the string, allow the twists to wind and unwind, wind again in the opposite direction, unwind, and so forth, with a rhythmic pressure of the hands and arms outward, in front of the body, almost as though you are playing an accordion.

You can wrap the cord directly around each hand, but this can present

a problem for small children (or even for grown-ups, come to that). If the thread or cord gets too tightly wrapped around the fingers, it can give a pretty firm pinch during the winding cycle. The larger the wheel, the stronger the pinch. For this reason, I've designed my color wheel with short pieces of dowel as protective handles. This way, the cord winds against them, not against your fingers.

One last tip, if you store the color wheel with the strings fully wound, it will set off right away with the first pull of the handles.

How to Make the Toy

1 Draw a 2-in.-radius circle on a scrap of ⅜-in. or ¼-in. plywood. Cut the disc 1/16 in. oversize, and then true up the circle with broad files and sandpaper, working from coarse to fine grits.

If you want the color wheel to be perfectly round, you can true up the disc on a lathe. First, make a glue block to attach to the disc (this way, you won't have to make a hole in the center of the disc). Cut a 1¼-in.-square glue block of ¾-in. pine and drill a ⅜-in.-diameter hole in the center. Now glue a 1¾-in.-long piece of ⅜-in. dowel in the

COLOR WHEEL

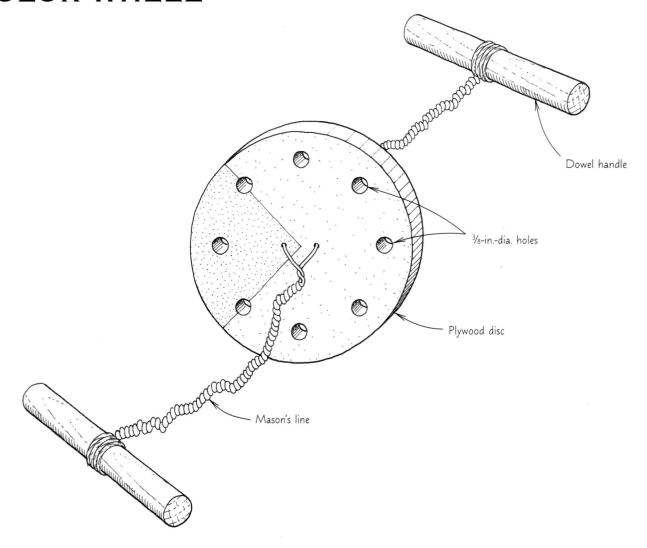

Dowel handle

³⁄₈-in.-dia. holes

Plywood disc

Mason's line

hole, and glue the block to the center of the disc with four small drops of glue. Clamp and let dry. Tighten the dowel firmly in the headstock chuck, turn the disc, and then sand. Remove the workpiece from the chuck, and separate the block from the disc with a sharp chisel. Sand away any remnants of the pine block.

2 Drill two $\frac{1}{16}$-in.-diameter holes along a diameter of the circle, each $\frac{5}{16}$ in. from the center.

3 Fill any voids in the plywood with wood filler and remove any sharp wood fibers from around the two holes with sandpaper. (Fibers gradually cut into the string.)

4 To add a whooshing sound effect to the spinning disc, drill eight $\frac{3}{8}$-in.-diameter holes equally spaced around a $1\frac{1}{4}$-in. radius. Place a block of wood under your plywood where the drill bit will exit to prevent the plywood from splitting.

5 Finish the wheel as you please—I used bright-colored acrylic paints. To make a vibrant orange, use three or four times as many total square inches of red as yellow paint; to make a strong green, use two or three times the blue.

Letting a child paint his or her own color wheel is a nice way to teach some of the attributes of color blending. You'll find that kids soon tire of producing gloppy, mud-colored mixtures.

6 Thread the mason's line through the two small holes near the center of the wheel. A 4-in.-diameter disc spins well on a 5-ft. total length of mason's line (or equivalent); this length includes four loops (a double clove hitch) around each handle. The handles end up about 2 ft. apart. Adjust the length of the loop (and the size of the color wheel) to match your child.

Folk Yo-Yo

Everyone's familiar with the two-disc yo-yo you can buy at any toy store, but this version's a little different. It works on the same principle as its commercial cousin, rising and falling on a string, but the string attaches at two points to a crossbar that goes right through the single disc.

Whether one disc or two, the toy is simple, but the derivation of "yo-yo" is surprisingly hard to track down. I had read that yo-yos were brought to America from the orient by child-loving seamen on the clipper ships, so it seemed probable that this strange word boasted an oriental origin. I looked up "yo-yo" in *Webster's Third International Dictionary*, but this trusted source simply reiterated what I already knew—that the yo-yo was a thick, grooved double disc with a string attached to its center "that is made to fall and rise to the hand by unwinding and rewinding on the string." No etymology, no derivation.

A recent *Encyclopedia Britannica,* in all the authority of its 44 million words, yielded "yoyo: Korean verse form of the late Koryo dynasty (935–1392), composed of six-line stanzas and dealing mainly with the theme of love." Not quite on the mark.

Finally, Antonia Fraser, in her fine book, *A History of Toys,* brought the shadowy yo-yo into the semblance of light:

"The yo-yo was known in the Far East in the most ancient times, and in the Philippines was actually used as a weapon, its user hiding in a tree, and striking his victim lethally on the head…. As the 'emigrette,' the yo-yo swept France…in the 1790's." By the 1920's it had swept America and the world, prompting a Persian newspaper to denounce the "dangerous toy" imported from the United States as "a time-wasting and immoral novelty."

FOLK YO-YO

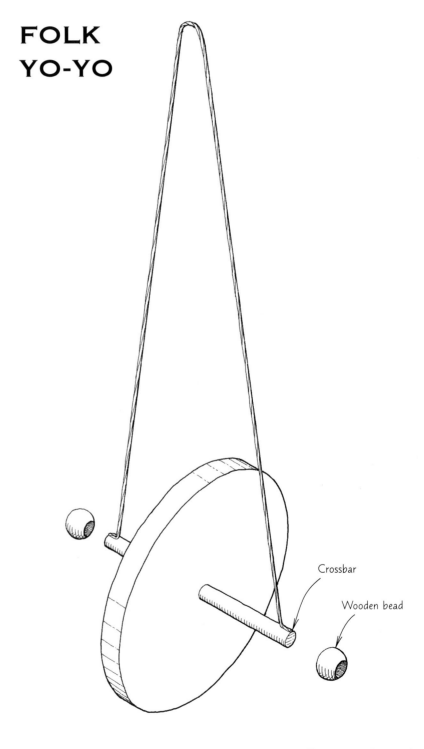

Crossbar

Wooden bead

2 Cut out the disc ¹⁄₁₆ in. oversized, and then true up the circle with broad files and sandpaper, working from coarse to fine grits. (You can also true up the disc on a lathe, as explained on pp. 59-61.)

3 Drill a ⅜-in.-diameter hole as perpendicular as possible in the center of the disc. Use a square to guide the drill, as explained on p. 40.

4 Paint the disc with your favorite design. I painted one side with a spiral pattern and the other with a floral design (see the patterns on the facing page).

5 Paint or varnish a 6-in.-long piece of ⅜-in.-diameter dowel.

6 When the disc is dry, insert the dowel in the hole and glue carefully, using a square to check that the dowel is at 90° to the disc.

7 Use about 36 in. of mason's line or other stout string as a cord. Glue the cord to the crossbar as you slide on the end caps made from large wooden beads or ⅞-in.-diameter dowel. (If you use dowel, round the ends so the string does not wind on the end cap.)

It takes a little time to get the hang of the single-disc yo-yo. Go slowly, winding the yo-yo to the top by hand, and then holding the string centered over the top of the disc. "Bump" the string upward as the yo-yo hits bottom, just as you would a two-disc yo-yo, and it will gradually climb the two strings. Manipulate your fingers to keep the strings away from the disc's sides.

The origins of the folk yo-yo pictured here are unclear. What is clear is that it descends and climbs a string with an elegance, smoothness, aplomb, and flash of color that will surprise you.

How to Make the Toy

1 Using a compass, draw a circle with a 4-in. radius on a piece of ¾-in.-thick plywood. You may want to try several sizes and thicknesses of wood (a smaller yo-yo is shown in the photo above). Push down on the point of the compass to make it easy to locate the exact center of the circle.

FOLK YO-YO

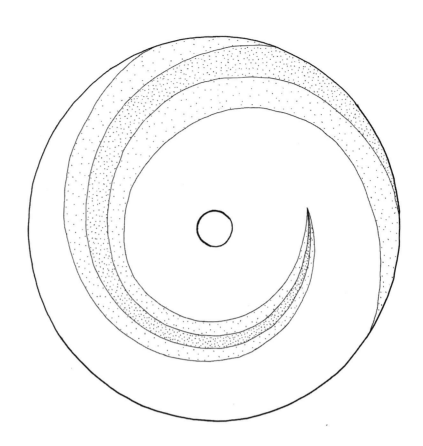

PATTERNS

Ariadne's Block

In Greek mythology, Ariadne was daughter of Pasiphae and Minos, king of Crete. As with most classical beauties, she fell in love, more specifically with the great soldier Theseus. As a woman of intelligence and practical skills, she helped Theseus escape from the horrendously complex Labyrinth after he had slain a creature half man and half bull called the Minotaur. Her method? She unrolled a ball of yarn or twine from the entrance of the Labyrinth until she met Theseus, and then escaped the Labyrinth by following it backward until they both reached the outside.

This folk toy, which exists in round, square, hexagonal, and octagonal forms, celebrates Ariadne's ability to get back to a starting point by following a string backward. To play the game (one or two persons can participate), push the needle through the holes in any pattern you wish—up, down, around, kitty-cornered—and then when there's no twine left, try to get back to the starting point.

Even though Ariadne possessed both great beauty and a sharp mind, they did not guarantee her much happiness. Her life after the famous follow-the-string-backward escape exists in four variations: (a) she was abandoned and hanged herself; (b) she died in childbearing on the island of Cyprus; (c) she was carried to the island of Naxos, where she died; or (d) while on Naxos she met and married the god of wine, Dionysus. (There's a striking bas-relief of Dionysus and Ariadne on display in the Vatican Museum, Rome.)

How to Make the Toy

You can make this little toy out of almost any wood. I started with some scraps of maple and mahogany, glued them together, and cut them in the miter box to make an octagon shape. Why an octagon? Because you can clamp a scrap of wood at the flat point where your drill exits, and thereby avoid splintering. (Squares and hexagon designs also work well.)

1 Glue the wood scraps together. I used three pieces, sandwiching the lighter maple between two scraps of mahogany.

2 Clamp the glued-up block in a miter box and cut all the 90° angles, including the top and bottom. Use a sharp cross-cut saw.

3 Cut the 45° angles (i.e., the four corners). Clamp the wood firmly to the miter box.

4 Drill ⅜-in. holes through the block in any pattern you like—just make sure they exit on a flat surface. Clamp a narrow piece of scrap over the exit hole to minimize splintering. Drill a ³⁄₃₂-in. hole for the mason's line or thin cord.

5 Sand the block smooth, rounding over the hard edges, and then apply a finish. (I used canola oil on this toy.)

ARIADNE'S BLOCK

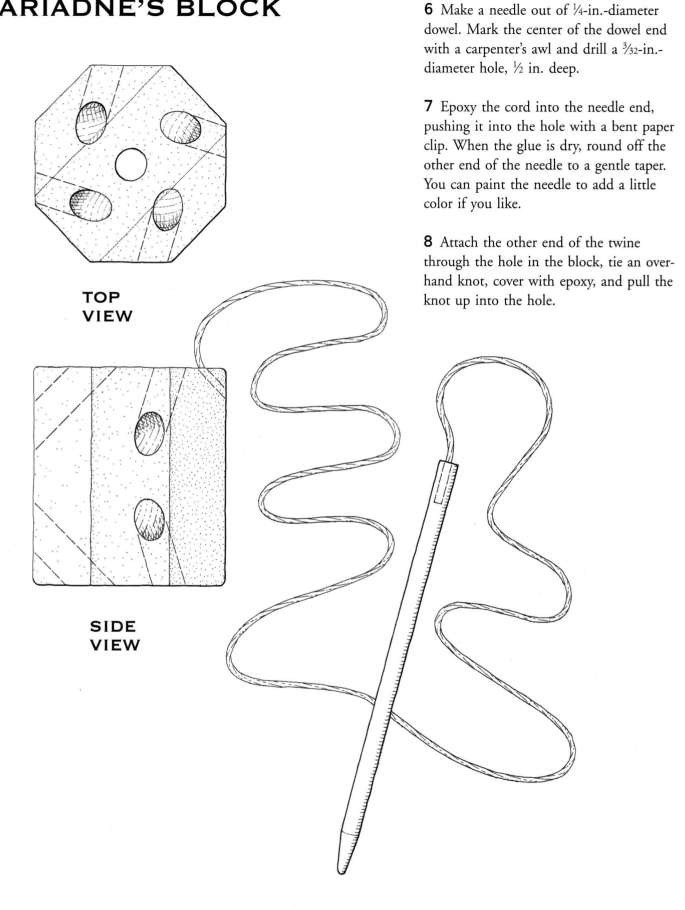

**TOP
VIEW**

**SIDE
VIEW**

6 Make a needle out of ¼-in.-diameter dowel. Mark the center of the dowel end with a carpenter's awl and drill a ³/₃₂-in.-diameter hole, ½ in. deep.

7 Epoxy the cord into the needle end, pushing it into the hole with a bent paper clip. When the glue is dry, round off the other end of the needle to a gentle taper. You can paint the needle to add a little color if you like.

8 Attach the other end of the twine through the hole in the block, tie an over-hand knot, cover with epoxy, and pull the knot up into the hole.

Will-o'-the-Wisp

I've seen several variations of this amusing folk toy, with clowns, acrobats, and curvilinear shapes as the sliding figure, but this one is my favorite. Since he's only a diminutive, smiling head, I decided one day to call him "Will-o'-the-Wisp," and the name stuck. It's almost impossible to walk by the toy without giving the quizzical little head a run down the angled pegboard (if you have the space, you can extend the inclined board to lengthen Will's run). It's an ideal project if you have only a few scraps of wood and dowel on hand and want to make a quick and interesting toy. Best of all, kids seem to love Will and the strange rhythmic movements of his head as gravity propels him downward.

How to Make the Toy

1 Cut out the base and the slide, using hardwood for the slide if you have it. Sand the pieces smooth with 100- and then 220-grit sandpaper, paying particular attention to the surface of the slide.

2 The key to the success of this toy is accurate positioning of the dowel pegs. Lay out the locations for the dowel holes on the slide either by careful measuring (using the slide pattern on p. 72 as a guide) or by transferring a photocopy of the pattern to the workpiece. Mark the location for each dowel hole with a carpenter's awl—the awl hole ensures that the drill bit doesn't wander. Carefully drill ¼-in.-deep holes at 90° to the slide.

3 Cut the 3/16-in.-diameter dowel to 1-in. lengths and glue in place with a drop of woodworker's glue. Wipe off any excess glue.

4 Transfer the pattern of the head to a piece of 1/2-in. hardwood and cut out. Because Will is rather small, you may wish to attach a small drum sander to a 3/8-in. drill to bring him to final shape.

5 Drill two holes in Will to receive the two small pieces of 1/4-in.-diameter dowel that serve as arms. The angle of the dowels is very important, so make sure to drill the holes at the angle shown on the pattern. Glue the dowels in place. (If necessary, you can trim or sand the dowels to length after a trial run.)

6 Paint Will's face with acrylic enamel, using my design or your own.

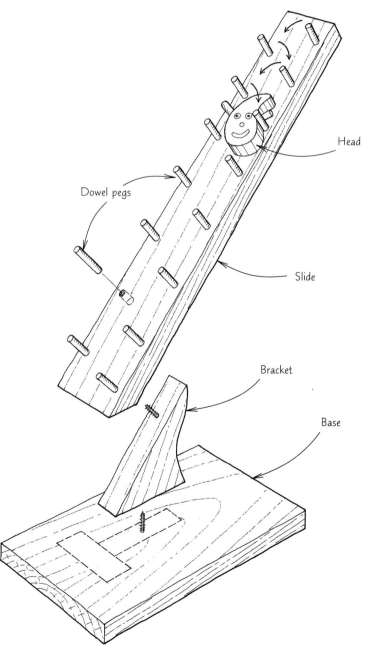

Head

Dowel pegs

Slide

Bracket

Base

WILL-O'-THE-WISP

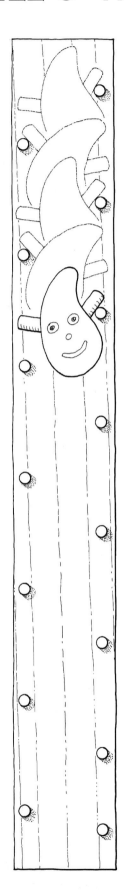

SLIDE

7 Finish all the parts with two coats of spar or polyurethane varnish, sanding between coats with 220-grit sandpaper.

8 Before you attach the slide to the base, try Will on a test run. Experiment with several slide angles until he descends at an optimum speed with a consistent rocking movement (I find that about 50° works well). Transfer the optimum angle to a piece of cardboard cut to size. Then trace the angle onto the bracket stock and cut the bracket to size. Cut the bottom of the slide to this angle, so that it meets flush with the base.

9 Glue and screw the bracket to the slide and the base to the bracket.

PATTERNS

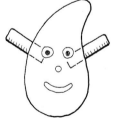

Scale
63%
Enlarge
160%

HEAD

BRACKET

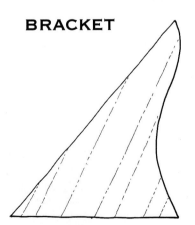

Stilts

When we think about stilts, we automatically picture parades, circuses, and children having fun. But stilts were originally made for serious uses—to allow adults to cross marshes and rivers before the advent of all-terrain vehicles.

There's a great stilt tale out of Belgian history. It seems that in the city of Namur at the time of the Renaissance, the two principal rivers, the Meuse and the Sambre, overflowed constantly, making ordinary foot traffic precarious, if not impossible. At the turn of the 17th century, the Governor of Namur, knowing his citizens' long-term facility with stilts, promised Archduke Albert of Belgium a detachment of soldiers who would move rapidly but "would not ride or walk." Curious, the Governor asked to see this phenomenon and upon viewing a skilled group of military men zipping by on stilts was so tickled by what he saw that he canceled permanently the tax on beer for all Namur citizens. Apparently there was great celebration at the news.

How to Make the Toy

These stilts are designed to be made from a single 8-ft. 2x4. Choose the hardest straight-grained, knot-free spruce, or even better, fir, you can find.

1 Custom-cut the length of the stilts to fit your child. A good rule of thumb is to make them up to your child's ears (when the child is standing on the ground).

2 Rip the cut piece in half along its length. Round over the top 18 in. or so of each stilt leg using a plane and a broad file followed by 150-grit sandpaper on a sanding block. When you are finished, each leg should look like a rather long wheelbarrow handle.

3 Transfer the footrest pattern to the 2x4 stock, and cut out two footrests

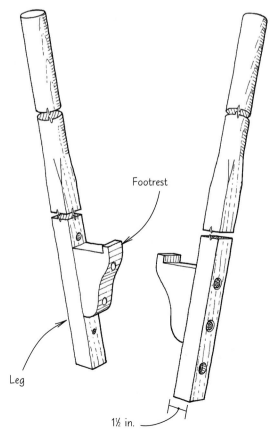

Footrest

Leg

1½ in.

(with the grain of the footrest running parallel to the stilt for greatest strength).

4 Each footrest is designed to attach with one 4½-in. and one 3½-in. lag bolt. Drill two ¼-in. holes for the bolts in each footrest. For additional support, also drill a 1-in.-deep hole for a ¾-in. dowel. Glue the 2-in.-long dowel into the hole with woodworker's glue.

5 Drill matching holes in the stilts, countersinking the back of the bolt holes. You can make just one footrest setting, but there's a certain advantage to drilling additional holes at greater heights so you can raise the footrests as the child grows.

6 Paint the footrests a bright color, and finish the stilt legs with spar varnish.

7 Assemble the footrests to the stilt legs with two lag bolts, nuts, and washers and the 2-in. dowel support.

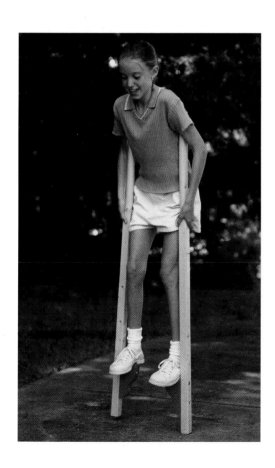

STILTS

PATTERN

Scale 48%
Enlarge 210%

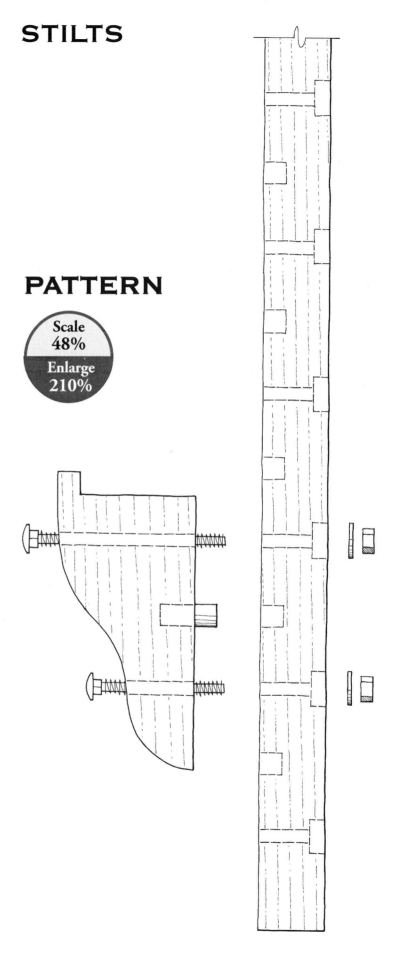

Man on the Edge

This intriguing folk toy is said to have its roots in Canada and came into this country by way of Idaho. It's one of many similar designs that rest on the edge of a table or a shelf and rock back and forth for a long time when given a gentle push. I've seen clowns, sawyers with up-and-down saws, and W. C. Fields-like topers—all looking as though they're going over the edge and then righting themselves thanks to the counterweight that hangs under the table or shelf. The physics of their stability is such that they nod back and forth within the same limits regardless of the weight of the block of wood, rock, or piece of lead that acts as the counterweight. A heavier weight (within reason) just makes them go for a longer time.

How to Make the Toy

1 Transfer the body pattern onto a piece of ¾-in.-thick hardwood. Cut out the body with a coping saw or sabersaw and cut or file the bottom of each leg to a wedge shape, with no more than ¹⁄₁₆ in. width at the bottom. This narrow dimension allows the Man on the Edge to rock back and forth with minimum friction.

2 Drill ³⁄₁₆-in.-diameter through holes for the eyes and a ¼-in.-diameter hole for the mouth. Drill a ⁵⁄₁₆-in.-diameter hole ½ in. deep below the head to hold the counterweight mechanism.

3 Transfer the arm patterns to ⅛-in. plywood (I used the wood from a small tangerine crate). Drill pilot holes for ½-in. headed brads in the upper arms and in the shoulders of the body.

- 1 piece 8½-in. x 2¼-in. x ¾-in. hardwood (body)
- 2 pieces 3½-in. x 1-in. x ⅛-in. plywood (arms)
- 15-in. length of ⁵⁄₁₆-in.-dia. hardwood dowel
- block, ball, or bead (connector piece)
- two ½-in. headed brads
- weight
- 30-in. length of twine

4 Apply two coats of varnish to all wooden parts, sanding smooth with 150-grit paper between coats.

5 Nail the arms to the body, leaving at least ¹⁄₁₆-in. clearance between the arm and the brad head so the arms swing freely.

6 Make the three-part counterweight holder from a length of ⁵⁄₁₆-in.-diameter hardwood dowel. It really doesn't matter what shape the connector piece is—it could be a cube, an odd-shaped block, or anything that's drillable—as long as the angle between the dowels is right. (I turned a maple ball on a lathe, but you could also use a large bead.) Mark the two hole locations on the connector piece with a carpenter's awl at as close to 75° as you can. Use a cardboard template cut to the correct angle to guide you.

7 Drill two holes ½ in. deep in the connector piece. (When drilling into a round ball, mark the location of the hole with a carpenter's awl and drill straight down from the top, holding the ball in a C-clamp.)

MAN ON
THE EDGE

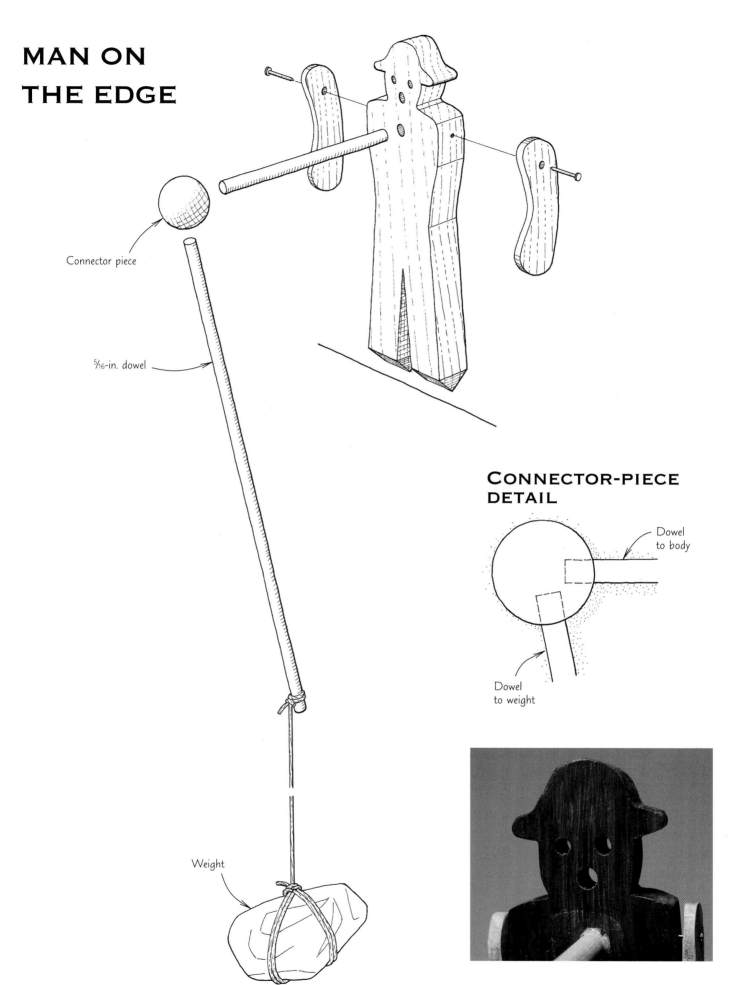

Connector piece

5/16-in. dowel

CONNECTOR-PIECE DETAIL

Dowel to body

Dowel to weight

Weight

8 Drill a 3/32-in.-diameter hole for the twine in the end of the long piece of dowel.

9 Glue the short dowel to the connector piece, but only dry-fit the longer piece at this stage (you may want to adjust the length after you've tested the toy). If necessary, use a paper shim to keep the loose dowel in place.

10 Use a rock, a large lead fishing sinker, a block of hardwood, or whatever is at hand for the counterweight. Thread the twine through the hole in the long dowel and secure with an overhand knot; add a dab of glue to the knot to prevent it from unraveling.

Attach the twine to the counterweight. If you're using a piece of rock, wrap the twine tightly two or three times around the girth and knot. Glue both the knot and the twine to the counterweight. If you're using a block of wood or lead, a screw eye makes an easy attachment.

11 Set the man on the edge of a table and give the weight a gentle push. If the figure leans forward too much so that at rest he is poised well out in the air, lengthen the longer piece of dowel. In the unlikely event the figure doesn't lean far enough, shorten the longer piece of dowel.

When you're happy with the setting, glue the dowel into the connector piece. The man should rock back and forth in a gentle, rhythmic motion, and the arms should spin wildly in the manner of a person desperately seeking to recover balance!

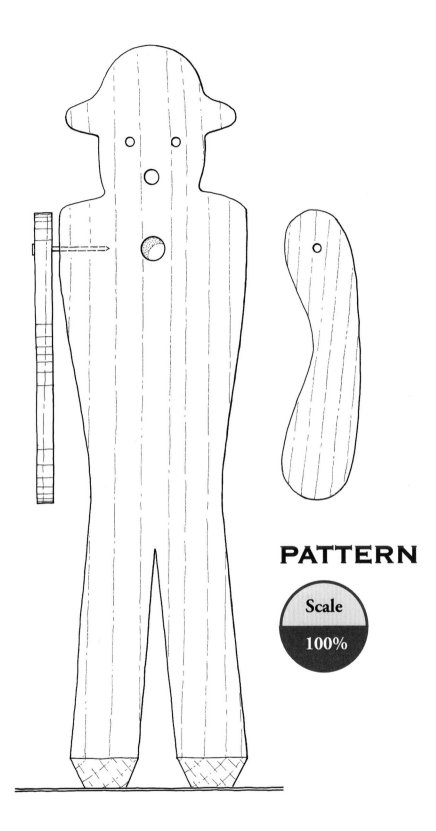

PATTERN

Scale

100%

Limberjack

The first time I saw someone with a limberjack was many years ago in a folk club in Freiburg, southern Germany. A young American singer had a small wooden dancing man cavorting in front of her, and she was captivating an audience with the dancer's antics and syncopations as well as with her own rendition of an Appalachian song. Everyone in the audience loved her wee dancing fellow, and I suddenly felt quite homesick.

Limberjacks came to America in the 19th century with the Irish, who used them not only as toys but also to accompany Celtic music; they were also painted black to imitate performers in minstrel shows. The limberjack's roots apparently go back into Scandinavian and central European culture. The name "limberjack," which plays on the word "lumberjack," probably derives from *limber,* meaning supple or agile, and *jack,* a common name for a sailor (jack-tar), a clown, or a common man (steeplejack).

To make the limberjack dance, put one end of the plywood springboard a few inches under your bottom while sitting on a hard chair. Holding the limberjack with the support dowel out toward the end of the springboard, flex his legs slightly downward and, with a couple of fingers or the side of your free hand, start beating out an interesting rhythm on the inner part of the springboard. The limberjack should start dancing to whatever tune you are beating out. His arms will often describe whole joyous circles, and he'll also dance with one leg well forward, the other well back, in a sort of semi-split, while rapping out a syncopated rhythm.

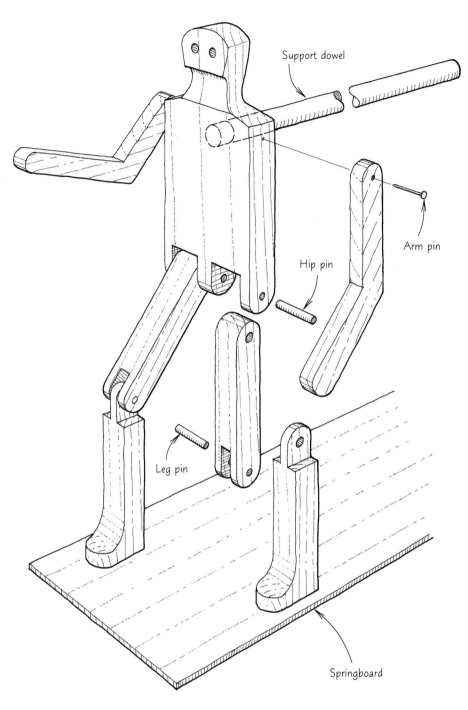

Support dowel

Arm pin

Hip pin

Leg pin

Springboard

- one 6-in. square of ½-in. hardwood, or other configuration of 36 sq. in., at least 2 in. wide (body and legs)
- one 4-in. square of ¼-in. hardwood (arms)
- two ⅝-in.-long headed brass brads (arm pins)
- 4-in. length of ⅛-in. maple dowel (leg and hip pins)
- 16-in. length of ⅜-in. maple dowel (support)
- 1 piece 20-in. x 3½-in. x ⅛-in. plywood (springboard)

How to Make the Toy

The limberjack should be made from hardwood. There are two reasons why: First, the arms need the strength of a close-grained wood, and, second, the toy operates better with the additional weight of a hardwood like cherry, ash, or maple. I've always preferred to make limberjacks of cherry and leave them unpainted, mainly because I like the contrast between the cherry body and the light-colored dowel and springboard.

1 Transfer the pattern of the body and legs to a piece of ½-in.-thick hardwood.

2 Transfer the arm pattern (times 2) to a piece of ¼-in. hardwood. The grain must go across the joint of the elbow and not straight down the upper arm or forearm; otherwise, the arm will break.

3 Cut everything to within 1/16 in. of the line and finish with a broad file or disc sander and emery boards. True up the neck cut with a small sanding drum mounted in a ⅜-in. drill. (Hardwood is slower to sand than pine, so it really helps to use a power sander on this toy.)

4 Drill three ⅛-in.-diameter holes in the body through the hips to receive a ⅛-in.-diameter dowel 1¾ in. long. This single dowel will pin both upper legs in place. While you still have the ⅛-in. bit in the drill, stack the upper legs exactly over each other and drill a ⅛-in. hole through both knee joints.

5 Drill a 9/64-in.-diameter hole through the upper legs at the hip joint and through the lower legs at the knee joint. If you don't have a 9/64-in. drill bit, you can wiggle the ⅛-in. drill bit while it is running to enlarge the hole very slightly. (These holes need to be a little larger than the holes in the body and the upper-leg knee joints so the legs will swing freely.)

6 Drill a 1/16-in.-diameter hole through the upper arm at each shoulder, and wiggle the drill bit very slightly to enlarge the hole. Drill a 1/16-in. pilot hole for the brad in the shoulder.

7 Drill 5/32-in.-diameter eyeholes. (Make sure they are carefully aligned, or the limberjack will look demented.)

8 Assemble the limberjack, using dowel pins that are slightly overlong. Glue neatly, keeping the glue away from the inner parts of the joints. When the glue is dry, sand the dowels flush.

9 Attach the arms to the body with 1/16-in.-diameter brass brads.

10 Cut an 18-in. length of ⅜-in. dowel as a support. Drill a ⅜-in.-diameter hole ⅜ in. deep in the limberjack's upper back to receive the dowel; center the hole 3/16 in. below a line drawn between the brads that hold the arms. Use a twist drill or a Forstner bit to make the hole, but not a spade bit (its point would emerge through the limberjack's chest).

PATTERNS

Scale
77%

Enlarge
130%

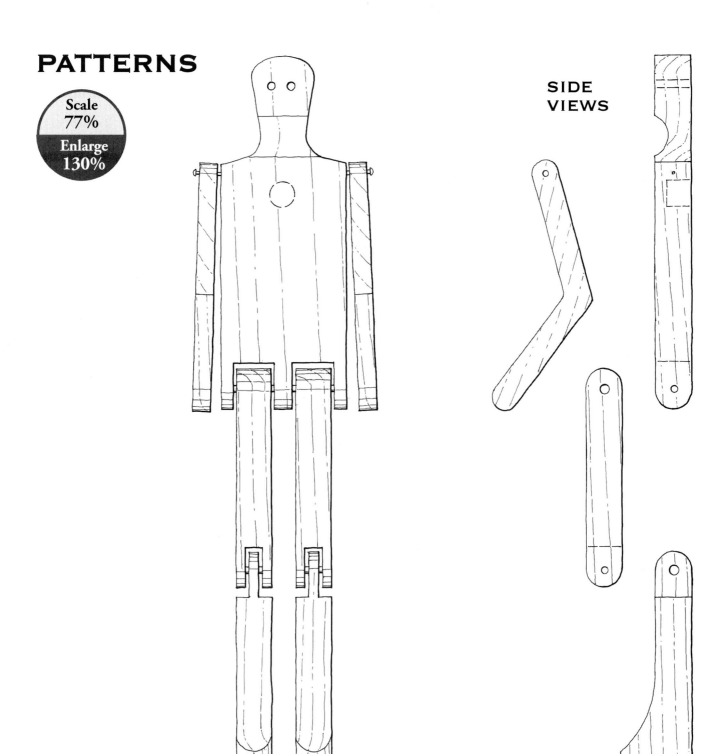

SIDE
VIEWS

11 Insert the dowel in the body, using a paper shim if necessary to hold it tight.

12 Sand the limberjack with 180-grit paper, and then finish everything with two coats of 50% boiled linseed oil and 50% turpentine. Rub with a soft

cloth after the finish has soaked into the wood.

13 Make a springboard of ⅛-in.-thick plywood. (I used a scrap culled from the skin of a birch-plywood, hollow-core door.)

Rollo the Magnificent

High-wire acrobats are notorious attention-getters, and Rollo is no exception. If you set him on a piece of string stretched a foot or so below the ceiling of a child's room, he will balance there with a miraculous equipoise. Watching the world from his lofty perch, he defies gravity, inviting the admiration of groundlings, no matter what their age.

Alternatively, you can rig up a long line outside between a tree and your house and watch Rollo speed across your backyard, rocking and rolling on his way. His speed is controlled by the amount one end of the line is attached higher than the other. If you give Rollo and a long length of mason's line to a couple of kids, you can be sure they'll come up with some new way to play with this happy little fellow.

Rollo is one of those toys whose origins completely baffle me, but I would guess that the original model is probably 150 years old. Construction is simple: As with many other folk toys, the original toymaker has replaced the legs and feet with a wheel—Rollo's turns on a ¼-in.-diameter axle. His weights can be made of either softwood or hardwood, and he's very rugged. Considering the small investment in construction time and the minimal cost, Rollo exemplifies perfectly the rough genius of folk toys.

How to Make the Toy

1 Cut out Rollo's body from hardwood (I used ½-in. maple scavenged from a lumberyard pallet). It's best to use ½-in. rather than ¾-in. stock to lighten the amount of mass above the wire that must be counterbalanced from below. Drill ³⁄₁₆-in.-diameter holes for the eyes,

WHAT YOU NEED

- **1 piece 6-in. x 2¼-in. x ½-in. hardwood (body)**

- **2½-in. length of ¼-in.-dia. dowel (axle)**

- **1-in.-dia. x ¾-in.-thick hardwood wheel**

- **two 12-in. lengths of ¼-in.-dia. dowel (arms)**

- **two 3-in.-dia. x 1½-in.-thick weights**

- **length of mason's line**

lining them up carefully, and starting the holes with an awl.

2 Drill the ¼-in.-diameter hole in the body for the axle, and then dry-fit the ¼-in. dowel axle (don't glue it yet).

3 There are a number of ways to make the wheel. If you have a lathe, turn the wheel from a scrap of hardwood (I used birch), making a ⅛-in.-deep groove in which the mason's line will run. Taking your time, drill a ⁹⁄₃₂-in.-diameter hole exactly perpendicular to the wheel. It's important to make the hole as accurate as possible so the wheel doesn't wobble too much in use.

If you don't have access to a lathe, cut out the wheel with a 1⅛-in.-diameter hole saw (which will leave a ¼-in.-diameter hole in the center of the wheel). Secure the wheel onto a 2¼-in.-long, ¼-in.-diameter bolt with two flat washers and a nut, and tighten the bolt end in the chuck of a ⅜-in. drill. Clamp the drill securely to a bench, and make a small chisel rest (from a scrap of wood approximately 3 in. by 2 in. by 1 in.) that will hold a chisel along the center-line of the chuck. Screw the chisel rest down about ⅛ in. from the wheel. Turn on the drill and cut in the groove

approximately ⅛ in. deep using a small chisel (or a sharpened large nail). Then, with the drill still running, smooth all surfaces of the wheel with an emery board. Drill out the ¼-in. center hole of the wheel to 9⁄32 in. diameter.

A third alternative is to buy two 1-in.-diameter wheels from a hobby shop, round over the edge on one side, and glue the two wheels together. The mating rounded-over edges will form the groove for the mason's line.

4 Test the fit of the wheel on the dowel axle; sand the dowel if the wheel binds at all. Then assemble the body, wheel, and axle, making sure you don't get any glue on the wheel so that it spins freely.

5 Drill holes for the arms at 45° to the body, marking the drill bit's starting point with an awl. To help drill the holes accurately, draw a centerline down the body and make 45° triangles of cardboard. Tape the triangles to the body and line them up with the centerline.

6 Dry-fit the ¼-in.-diameter dowel arms into the body.

7 Cut out the arm weights from hardwood, if you have it (though 1½-in.-thick construction lumber works almost as well). Drill a ¼-in.-diameter hole in the center of each weight. The weights should stay on the dowel arms by friction alone.

8 Stretch a length of smooth-finished mason's line tightly between two fixed points and set Rollo on the line. Adjust the weights (by sliding them up and down the arms) until he balances in a perpendicular position; be warned, it's difficult to get him to balance right off the bat. Trim any dowel that protrudes beyond the weight (or you can decrease the diameter of one weight slightly—no one will notice). Glue the dowels into the body, but don't glue the weights onto the dowels: In the event that Rollo crashes, the weights will slide up the arms and cushion the shock.

ROLLO THE MAGNIFICENT

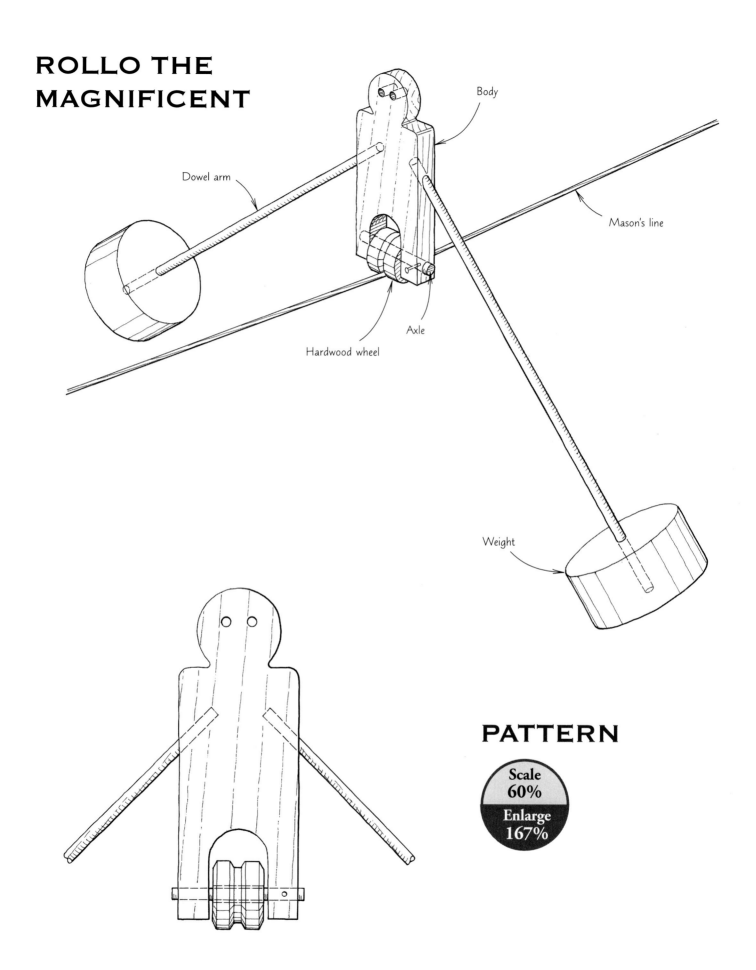

Body

Dowel arm

Mason's line

Axle

Hardwood wheel

Weight

PATTERN

Scale
60%

Enlarge
167%

Rolling Acrobat

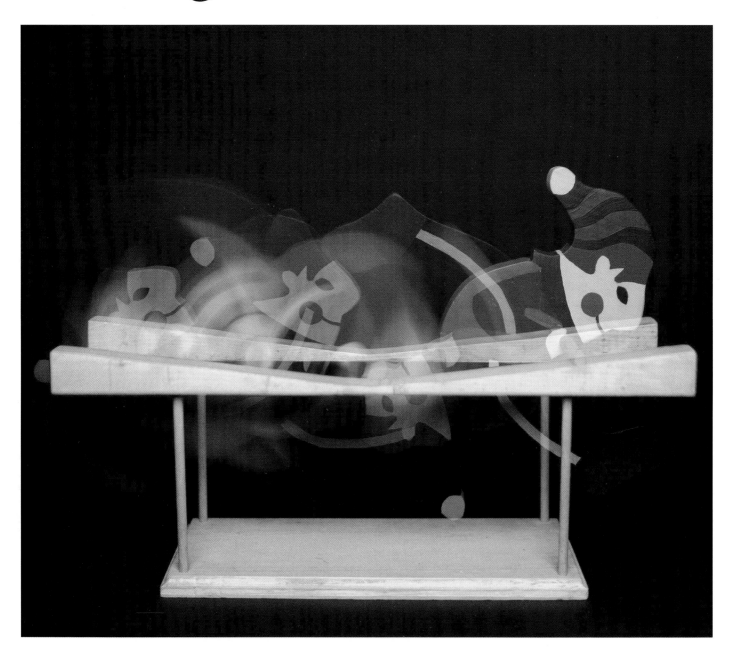

I chanced upon this energetic circus performer one summer evening when my family and I were sailing off the coast of Maine and dropped anchor in Stonington Harbor, off Deer Isle, and went ashore. A local craftsman was selling folk toys and home-crafted wooden gifts from his front lawn, and our two boys instantly fell in love with this brightly colored entertainer. Within moments, they began competing to see who could make the acrobat roll back and forth a greater number of times. The original toy was smaller than the one pictured here, but I discovered later that the design worked better at twice the original size.

There's a good deal of skill involved in getting the best performance out of this little acrobat. Try starting him about ½ in. from one end of the ramps with his legs parallel to the base, and rotate the dowel with your thumb and fore-

WHAT YOU NEED

- **1 piece 12-in. x 11½-in. x 1½-in. clear construction lumber (acrobat body)**

- **9-in. length of ⁷⁄₁₆-in.-dia. hardwood dowel (acrobat arms)**

- **1 piece 16-in. x 7½-in. x ¾-in. pine (base)**

- **24-in. length of clear 2x4 construction lumber (2 ramps)**

- **32-in. length of ⅜-in.-dia. hardwood dowel (4 ramp supports)**

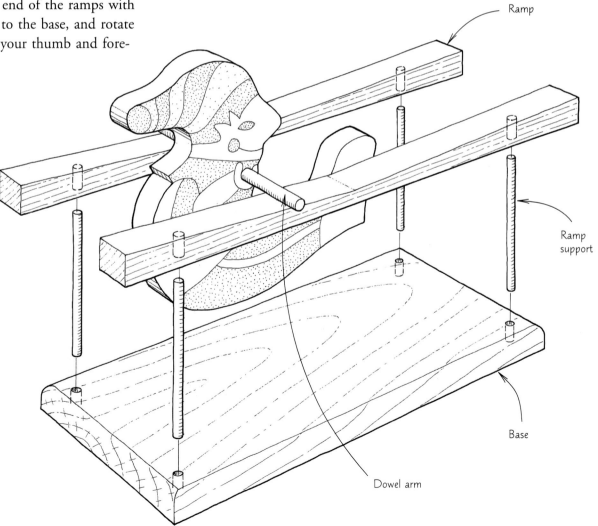

Ramp

Ramp support

Base

Dowel arm

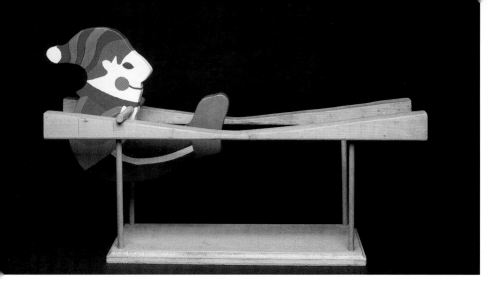

finger of each hand until he begins to roll. Count the number of passes back and forth until he stops. Then try starting him with his feet pointing straight up at the same ½ in. from the end. Experiment with his rotation so that he doesn't travel off the ramps but achieves the maximum number of revolutions possible. Our record is 14 passes (or 7 complete cycles) back and forth!

How to Make the Toy

1 Transfer the pattern of the acrobat body onto a piece of clear (knot-free) 1½-in.-thick pine or other construction lumber.

2 Cut out the body using a coping saw or sabersaw. (If you're using a coping saw, be sure to use a sharp blade and cut slowly in wood this thick.) Get to within ¹⁄₁₆ in. of the line with the saw, and then use a broad file to remove the rest of the wood to the line. Sand the entire piece with 150-grit paper.

3 Transfer the lines for the color scheme onto the acrobat's right side a second time (the first lines will have been erased by sanding) using a photocopy of the pattern and a hot iron.

With a soft pencil, trace the color scheme onto the other side of your photocopy, and then transfer this reverse image to the acrobat's left side so that you have color-scheme lines on both sides of the toy.

4 Paint the acrobat's body using acrylic paints and a medium-sized artist's brush (you'll probably need a fine-point ⅛-in. brush to paint some of the fine details). Two good coats should suffice, except for the yellow stripe, which I found required three coats to cover. The body has a fair number of complex curves; if you're not confident painting them freehand, use tape to mask off adjacent areas (as explained in the sidebar on p. 47).

5 Cut out the base from ¾-in. pine. Smooth the cuts with 50-grit followed by 120-grit broad files, and finish-sand with a sanding block.

6 Drill four ⅜-in.-diameter holes in the corners of the base, with each hole set back ¾ in. from each side (see the drawing on p. 89). Be careful to keep the drill and bit perpendicular to the base while drilling. Stop when the holes are ⅝ in. deep (it may be helpful to wrap a piece of masking tape around the bit at ⅝ in. to serve as a gauge).

7 Cut four pieces of ⅜-in.-diameter dowel, each 8 in. long.

8 Transfer the pattern of the ramp to a 24-in. length of clear 2x4 construction lumber. Dress down the final ¹⁄₁₆ in. of the ramps with 50-grit and 120-grit broad files, but don't sand the surface completely smooth. This toy rolls better when there is a slight roughness to the inclined surface and the dowel supporting the acrobat does not skid.

PATTERNS

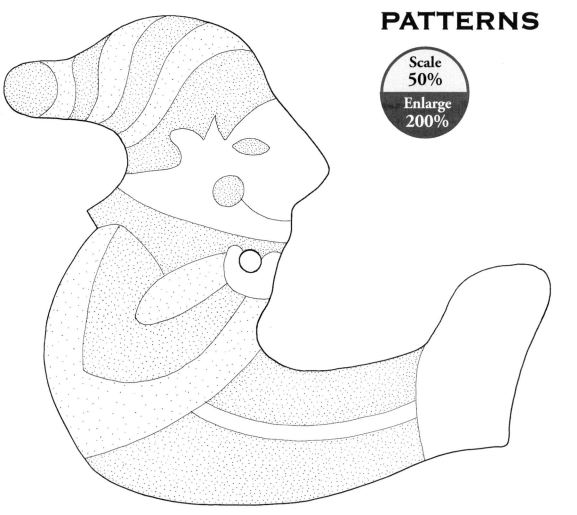

Scale
50%

Enlarge
200%

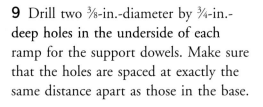

RAMP

Note: This pattern is for one-half of the ramp only. Flop the pattern for the other half of the ramp.

9 Drill two ⅜-in.-diameter by ¾-in.-deep holes in the underside of each ramp for the support dowels. Make sure that the holes are spaced at exactly the same distance apart as those in the base.

10 Assemble the base, the four dowels, and the two ramps. Apply a small amount of wood glue to the ends of each dowel. While the glue is still wet, make fine adjustments with a ruler or tape measure and a gentle touch with your hammer to make sure that the two ramps are parallel to the base. Set the assembly aside to dry.

11 Drill a ⁷⁄₁₆-in.-diameter hole in the acrobat for the dowel (place a block of scrap pine underneath the hole so the wood doesn't splinter as the bit exits). Make sure the hole is perpendicular to the acrobat and in exactly the place indicated on the pattern. Accuracy here will ensure that the acrobat balances properly. Insert and center a 9-in. length of ⁷⁄₁₆-in.-diameter dowel and glue in place.

12 For looks and durability, you may want to paint or stain the base, the four dowels, and the ramps (I stained mine a medium pine color). But don't paint the top surfaces of the ramps because it will make them too smooth and the dowels will skid as the acrobat rolls.

Two Early American Board Games

These two board games, Nine Men's Morris and Fox and Geese, were played as long ago as the late 18th century in America and are still a lot of fun both for children and adults. When I saw the games set up at Historic Deerfield, in Deerfield, Massachusetts, I was immediately struck by the "counters" or playing pieces. Both the nine men (painted and natural) and the geese were kernels of corn, and the fox was represented by a russet-colored dried bean. I can vouch for these games as low-tech entertainments, because no matter how carefully I searched, I couldn't find an on-off switch or a battery box hidden in either one.

Nine Men's Morris, also known as "mill," "the mill," "muhle," or "morelles," is one of the oldest of board games and was highly popular in Europe in the 1300s. It has roots going back at least to classical Greece, where its board pattern was discovered carved into the steps of the Acropolis at Athens. The name "Morris" probably derives from the game's fanciful resemblance to the Morris (Moorish) dance. The game was evidently brought to Revolutionary America by Hessian mercenaries, who, after they surrendered, probably taught it to their captors. In pre-Revolutionary America, the Puritans, of course, had disapproved of board games and playing cards, judging them frivolous or, worse, inventions of the dark one.

Fox and Geese probably originated in the Middle Ages and appears in the family records of the English king Edward IV (1461-1483) as "fox and hounds," with the counters cast in silver—a far cry from the later American kernels of corn. By the time of the American Revolution, Fox and Geese had spread over much of Western Europe, although the game varied in

WHAT YOU NEED

- **two 10-in. squares of ¾-in. pine (game boards)**
- **88-in. length of 1-in. x ¼-in. pine (borders)**
- **two ¾-in.- or 1-in.-long brass hinges**
- **small latch (optional)**
- **counters (marbles, kernels of corn, or similar)**

form. In France, for example, the game board had 37 holes instead of the more common 33. Some game boards were round, with ornamental carved feet and a deep groove cut around the circumference to hold the defeated geese.

How to Make the Game Board

1 Cut two 10-in. squares of ¾-in. pine. Clamp the squares together and sand with a broad file to make all four sides line up.

2 Transfer the game patterns (see p. 96) to the 10-in. squares with tracing paper and carbon paper or a photocopy and a very hot iron.

3 Cut the game boards' lines into shallow grooves in the wood: This operation is not difficult, but it does take a little patience. Using a utility knife with a sharp blade guided by a straightedge, you need to make three cuts along each line with medium pressure on the blade. For the first, cut straight down on the line; for the second, move the straightedge ⅟₁₆ in. to one side and make a 45° angle cut, drawing the knife blade twice along the straightedge. Make all the first

BOARD GAMES

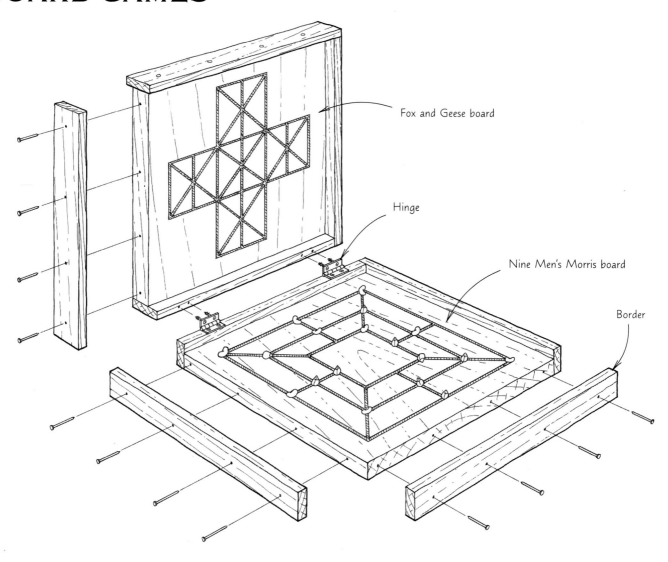

Fox and Geese board

Hinge

Nine Men's Morris board

Border

and second cuts on all the lines, and then turn the board 180° and cut the second side of the "V" on each line. Clean out the cut wood with the tip of your knife, and then score down on the groove with the tip of the blade to equalize the depth of the groove so far as possible.

4 Using the side of an emery board, sand each groove to a uniform profile.

5 Glue and nail on a 1-in. by ¼-in. border on each side of the 10-in. squares

(you'll need eight pieces in all). I was able to find small hinges for my box, but if you can't get ones with leaves narrower than ¼ in., use a thicker border (up to ½ in.) on the side that will receive the hinges. Butt the corners together, or for a better-looking box miter the corners.

6 Install the small brass hinges, making sure that the box's borders line up when the two halves are shut. For a nice touch, add a simple latch to keep the box together (not shown on my design).

7 Choose colors and an overall finish inside and out for the game board. I like orange shellac on pine because it gives the board an instant antique look. Colors used on the inside surfaces will contrast quite brilliantly with the shellac.

How to Play the Games

NINE MEN'S MORRIS

The 18 pieces or "counters" are divided into two groups of 9. Each group is a contrasting color (white and black or white and red are most common). The two players alternate playing the pieces on the board, one at a time. The aim is to make rows of three of the same color, while preventing your opponent from doing the same. Each piece must be placed on a "spot" or intersection, and each row of three must be along connecting lines.

Whenever you make a row of three of your own color, you may remove one of your opponent's pieces. However, you cannot take one of your opponent's pieces that is in a row of three if he or she has other pieces anywhere on the board that are not in a row of three. When all unattached pieces or pieces in twos have been taken, then you can capture pieces that are a part of three-in-a-row.

Once all the pieces have been placed on the board (see the photo above), you now begin to move them, alternating turns with your opponent. Alternate the pieces' movements, one at a time, in any direction along the connecting lines (you cannot jump between the lines). The object is to make new rows of three. Each time you make a new

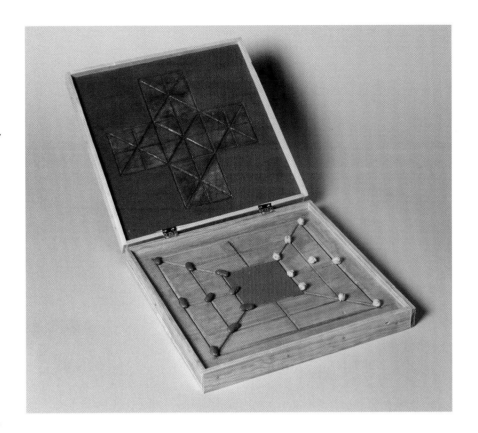

row of three, you may take your opponent's piece. The winner is the first to reduce his opponent to two pieces.

As an optional rule in games with children, when a player has only three counters left, he or she may get a second wind by moving any piece to any vacant point, regardless of connections.

FOX AND GEESE

One player (the fox) places one piece in the exact center of the board. The other player places 17 geese on the board on random intersections of the lines. The first move belongs to the fox, just as in nature, then one goose, and so on, with each player moving one piece at a time along the connecting lines, one intersecting "spot" at a time, in any direction.

The fox can jump, or "take," a goose whenever there is an empty spot behind the goose. The goose is then removed from the board. Just as in

checkers, the fox can make multiple jumps if empty spots appear behind a next adjacent goose.

But what hope exists for the teethless geese, since by the game's rules they cannot jump the fox? In just this: There is power (and safety) in numbers. They can surround the fox or force him into a corner. When the nimble fox can no longer jump, the geese win. When the geese can no longer corner the fox, usually when there are fewer than seven of their number remaining, the fox wins.

FOX AND GEESE

NINE MEN'S MORRIS

PATTERNS

Scale
40%
Enlarge
250%

Checkers

- one 12-in. square of ¾-in. plywood (board)

- 1 piece 16-in. x 20-in. x ¼-in. or ⅜-in. plywood (base)

- 84-in. length of 1-in. x ¾-in.pine (border)

- 14-in. length of 1¼-in.-dia. dowel (checkers)

- four ¾-in. flat-head steel screws

- twenty-four ¾-in. headed brads

I came across this checkerboard design at the Shelburne Museum of American Folk Art in Shelburne, Vermont, and loved its simplicity and practicality. It's long enough to span two sets of knees, it keeps the captured pieces right next to the board, and the squares are perfectly sized to take 1¼-in.-diameter checkers (which are easy to make using standard-sized closet rod).

How to Make the Game

Checkers, known as "draughts" in England, is one of the most ancient of all board games. It was played by the Egyptian pharaohs as long ago as 1600 B.C., but not until the 16th century A.D. was the game standardized throughout Europe on a 64-square board.

When I was a child, I used to play checkers with my mother on a thin wooden checkerboard that she and I would balance on our knees. I loved to play, but the setup had two distinct disadvantages. First, when you took your opponent's checkers or king, there was nowhere convenient to put the captured pieces, and they invariably got lost down the couch cushions. Second, because my mother was a much better player than I, it was all too easy to upset the flimsy board when it became absolutely clear that I was going to lose. (I think that my mother finally gave up playing with me after the checkers, board and all, hit the deck for the tenth time while I was pretending to swat a fly. Only now do I fully appreciate what that sweet woman went through with four sons.)

1 Start with a 12-in. by 12-in. square of plywood with at least one good side. Fill any voids with quick-drying wood putty and sand the top and edges smooth. Then paint the top and edges with two or three coats of red acrylic paint.

2 While the paint is drying, cut a piece of ¼-in. or ⅜-in. plywood measuring 16 in. by 20 in. for the base. Fill any voids (if you plan to paint the base) and sand the best side and edges thoroughly.

3 Cut a 1-in. by ¾-in. pine border to go around the edge of the plywood base. Using a miter box, cut the ends of the four border pieces at 45°. Glue all joints and nail and glue the base to the border from the underside with ¾-in. headed brads. Nail the corner joints of the border to keep them from coming apart.

4 Using a soft pencil, mark off 1½-in. squares on the checkerboard. Mask off every other row (horizontally and vertically) with tape and paint 16 squares with two coats of black; remove the masking tape while the paint is still tacky. When the paint is dry, mask and paint the squares in the rows in between.

CHECKERS

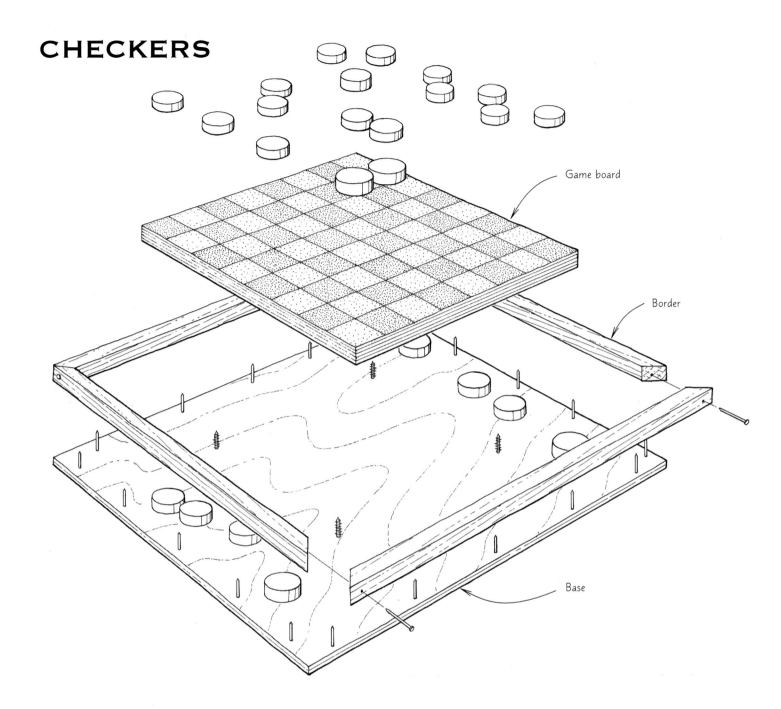

Game board

Border

Base

5 Center the 12x12 checkerboard on the plywood base and glue it down. When the glue is dry, screw from the underside with four ¾-in. flat-head steel screws. Countersink the screws.

6 Cut 26, ½-in.-thick discs (24 game pieces and 2 extras) with a fine-toothed crosscut saw from a 14-in. length of standard-sized closet rod (available at any hardware store). Butt the 1¼-in.-

diameter rod in your miter box against a stop, set to make sure each checker is ½ in. thick.

7 Paint the checkers. Traditional checker-set pieces are painted white and black or red and black. My piece of fir closet rod had a lovely grain, so I varnished one half of the discs (the "white" checkers) to show off the grain. The other half I painted with black acrylic.

Shoofly Rocking Horse

nquestionably among the most loved of all toys, rocking horses have been a childhood staple for centuries. They have been made in all shapes and sizes, from a monster that the English King George III commissioned to seat his family of four to miniatures for doll houses. Whether commissioned by kings for princes and princesses or fashioned from the humblest materials at hand by folk artists for their families, what unites them all is a fascination with the rocking motion, the horse in flight, the control over rocking (running) speed, the beauty of the horse pure and simple.

This particular rocking-horse design, with a seat between two identical side supports, is known as a "shoofly" rocker and is based on a design dating from the late 19th century. The original was

WHAT YOU NEED

- **2 pieces 30-in. x 18-in. x ¾-in. plywood (sides)**

- **2 pieces 11-in. x 9-in. x ¾-in. pine (seat and seat back)**

- **11-in. length of ¾-in.-dia. hardwood dowel (handgrip)**

- **1 piece 40-in. x 6-in. x ¾-in. hardwood (rockers)**

- **1 piece 12½-in. x 8½-in. x ¼-in. plywood (rocker brace)**

- **twenty-four 2½-in. drywall screws**

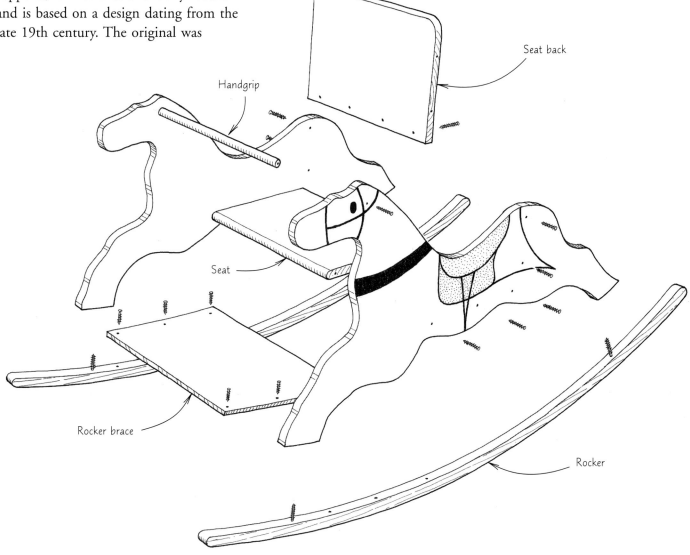

Seat back

Handgrip

Seat

Rocker brace

Rocker

made for a young child, with a comfortable seat and a close-to-the-ground security. How much was it used? The original hardwood rockers were worn down a full ¼ in. at the center. A long-standing folk tradition determined the color: dappled-gray horses were thought to bring good luck.

How to Make the Toy

1 Cut out two identical sides from ¾-in. plywood. Fill any voids in the laminates with wood putty. Round over all edges, except the bottoms of the hooves, with broad files and sandpaper.

2 Paint the sides a solid light color, and then add the saddle, the horse's eye, and other details of the harness work before assembling the horse.

3 Cut out the seat and the seat back from ¾-in. pine; sand smooth and paint or varnish before assembly.

4 Cut out the rockers from a strong hardwood—oak, ash, or hickory is a good choice. Clamp the rockers together and sand the bottoms until their profiles are identical; then sand all other surfaces smooth. Apply two coats of varnish, sanding between coats.

5 Make a handgrip from a length of ¾-in.-diameter hardwood dowel. Drill the dowel ends for 2½-in. drywall screws, and then paint the dowel with three coats of bright-red acrylic enamel.

6 Assemble all parts with countersunk drywall screws and woodworker's glue. (Using screws rather than nails will ensure the horse's long life.)

7 Fill the screw-head holes on the horse's sides with wood putty, and touch up with paint when dry.

SHOOFLY ROCKING HORSE

PATTERN

Scale 20%

Enlarge 500%

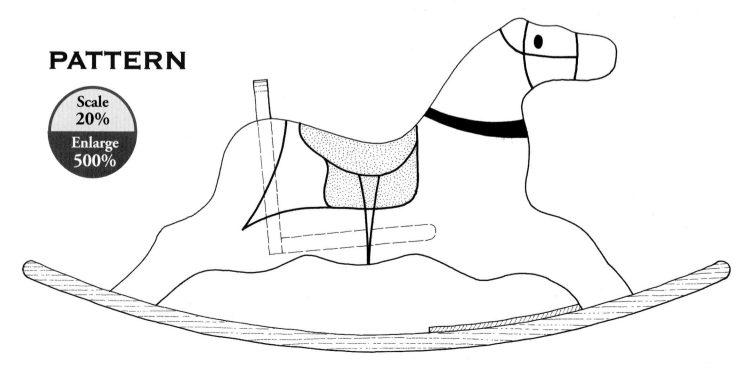

Building Blocks

Our family has always had a set of building blocks of one sort or another, probably because blocks are such a sure winner when children come to visit. Yet familiar as building blocks are, who knows when they were first conceived? If ever a toy's origins were irrecoverably lost in the murky mists of the past, it would have to be building blocks. Placing one small piece of wood, stone, brick, or dried clay on top of another to achieve height, balance, or multiple color effects, or to cast a different shadow—for how many millennia has this primal building up and tearing down gone on? You might as well ask when the opposable thumb first appeared.

The building-block set described here brought our two sons years of spirited construction and even more spirited destruction. I've made it anew with a matching box, which I should have done the first time around, because the box makes it easy to keep the blocks in order, and the container can become a part of the play materials. It also makes a sturdy little seat or a neat step for getting into forbidden territory.

A block set like this one has almost no material cost if you wear your recycler's hat and visit a local building site. Everything, including the plywood bottom for the box, the ¾-in. pine for the box's sides, 40 ft. of 2x4 scraps, and the thin material for the ramps, came from a single visit to a duplex under construction in our neighborhood. You'll want 28 usable feet of 1½-in. by 3-in. block material, so figure on about one-third waste and get 40 ft. to 48 ft. of 2x4 to begin with.

How to Make the Toy

The great appeal of this design is that everything fits together. The basic geometry is simple, based on the fact that all "two by" common framing lumber (2x4, 2x6, etc.) is actually 1½ in. thick.

Starting with this dimension, I made the basic width double that, or 3 in. So there are blocks 1½ in. by 3 in. by 3 in.; then double that length to 1½ in. by 3 in. by 6 in.; then double again in length to 1½ in. by 3 in. by 12 in.; and two designs of triangles, a few overpasses, some 1½-in. by 1½-in. by 6-in. pillars, and four 6-in. squares of ³⁄₁₆-in. plywood for roofs or ramps.

This is one toy where it really helps to have a table saw to do the ripping, although you can get by, albeit more slowly, with a handsaw.

If you don't want to do the ripping involved to get a true 3-in. width, you can make the block set out of 2x4 material, with a finished width of 3½ in. The set will work almost as well; you just won't have two material thicknesses equal one width. Blocks will be 3½ in. square, 7 in. long, and 14 in. long.

BLOCKS

1 Mark out blocks of 3 in., 6 in., and 12 in. on 2x4 stock to arrive at the least waste. You'll want to leave out damaged and dented wood and large or loose knots.

2 Cut the ends of all the blocks in a miter box to a true 90°. Squareness is very important: Blocks that are out of square will cause the building or tower walls to bulge out or collapse.

3 Rip each 2x4 block (actually 1½ in. by 3½ in.) down to 3 in. in width.

4 Make the specialty cuts (the hypotenuse of each triangle, the overpass semicircles) with a ripsaw, coping saw, or sabersaw.

5 Smooth all surfaces and put a small roundover on each edge with 120-grit sandpaper.

6 If you want, you can finish the blocks with varnish or oil to keep them clean, but no one will turn you in to the finish police if you leave everything au naturel (and the pine smells wonderful). Your kids will love them—just as long as they stack straight.

BUILDING BLOCKS

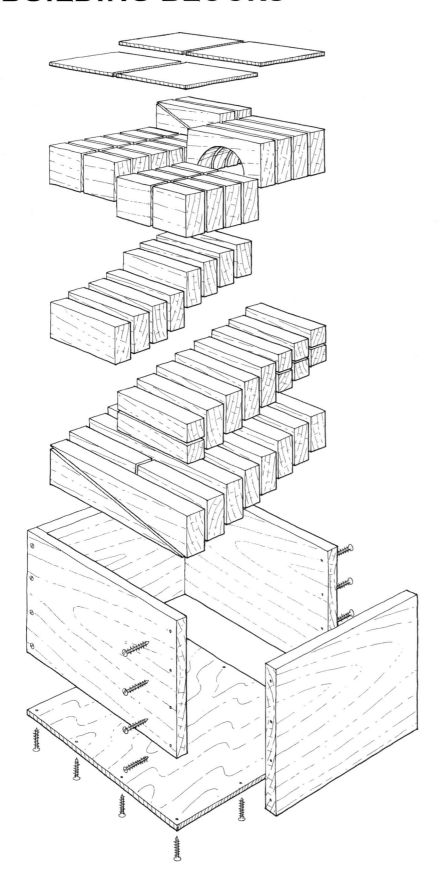

STORAGE BOX

Make the sides of the box of ¾-in.-thick pine or plywood, so that the inner dimensions measure 12½ in. square. The bottom, which overlaps the sides, is therefore 14 in. square. Pile up the blocks you've made in a solid 12-in. by 12-in. rectangular pile, and make the height of the sides correspond to your pile plus ½ in. Assemble the box with 2-in. drywall screws and glue. The four thin 6-in. by 6-in. ramps sit on top of the blocks, acting as a cover.

If you use full-width 2x4s for your blocks, make the inside dimension 14¾ in. square, with a 16¼-in.-square bottom. If you desire, finish the outside of the box with two coats of varnish.

Jacob's Ladder

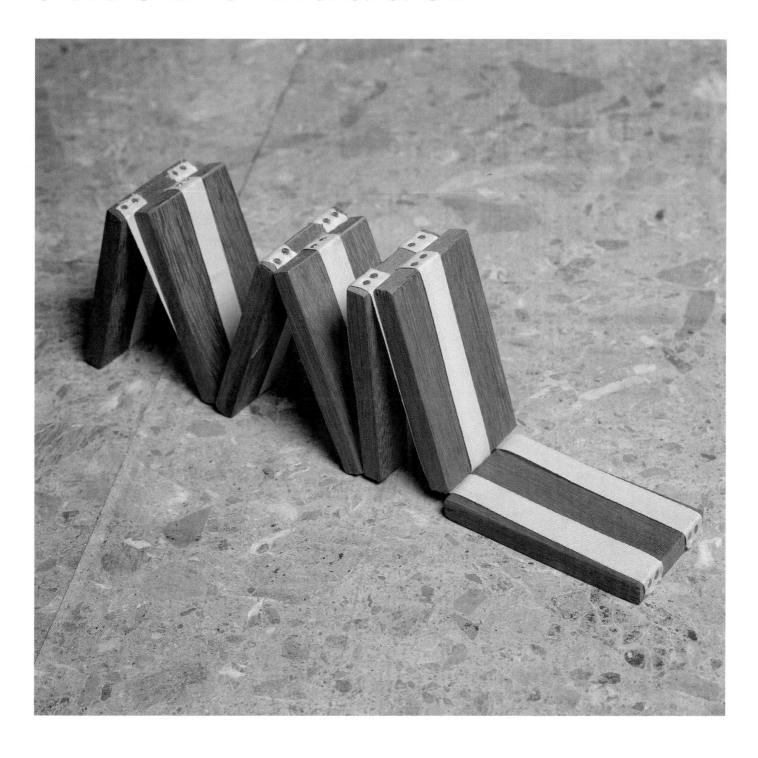

The Jacob's ladder is one of the most ancient and famous of folk toys. Legend has it that one was found in King Tut's tomb, which means these fascinating toys were played with in Egypt before 1352 B.C., when the young king died (at about 18 years old). It's amazing to me that this humble folk toy would have been included among Tutankhamen's most significant effects, along with brilliant jewelry, amulets, masks of pure gold, prized objets d'art, a solid gold coffin, statues, furniture, and even a full-sized chariot.

Jacob's ladders, named for the biblical Jacob who saw a ladder leading from earth to heaven in a vision, have shown up all over the world. Like the spinning top, the Jacob's ladder seems to be universal, appearing at widely divergent world locations with no apparent historical connectedness.

I still don't completely understand how this toy works. Engineer friends of mine have told me that the apparent falling of the blocks has to do with a double-acting hinge. But to name it is not to comprehend it. To operate the toy, simply hold the top block by its edges and let the rest of the identical blocks swing downward until the "ladder" is fully open. Then, holding the top block by its edges, turn it 180° in a left rotation, until the top and second blocks are parallel and touching. When the held block hits the hanging block, a series of blocks will begin cascading down. Then repeat the motion 180° to the right. Each time you move the block 180°, a cascade of apparently moving blocks will flip to the bottom.

There's a neat trick you can play with your Jacob's ladder, which will baffle children (and, most likely, their elders): Fold up a dollar bill into a small rectangle and tuck it under one of the tapes. Then operate the toy. The dollar will successively disappear, appear, disappear, and so on, for no apparent reason.

How to Make the Toy

I've seen plans that instruct you to glue the tapes to the bottom and top edges of the blocks. Don't trust them. I have reviewed several ways of making this toy, and I can assure you that gluing does not work. Glue often seeps into the tapes by capillary action, beyond the tops and bottoms of the blocks, and makes the tapes stiff; thus the toy runs poorly or not at all.

A better way is to attach the tapes with small headed brads—the larger and thinner the head, the better. The brads hold down the tapes sufficiently well in a simple attachment to the block, and the toy runs very smoothly.

1 Cut out six, seven, or eight rectangles measuring $3\frac{1}{2}$ in. by $1\frac{3}{4}$ in. from $\frac{3}{8}$-in.-thick hardwood or plywood. (The number of rectangles depends on the height of the child, or, more specifically, on the distance from the child's hand to the floor.)

WHAT YOU NEED

- **6, 7, or 8 blocks of $3\frac{1}{2}$-in. x $1\frac{3}{4}$-in. x $\frac{3}{8}$-in. hardwood or plywood**

- **10-ft. length of medium-weight binding tape**

- **$\frac{1}{2}$-in.-long headed brads**

2 If you're using plywood, fill any voids in the laminate with fast-drying wood putty, sand well with 180- or 220-grit sandpaper, and paint the blocks contrasting colors. If you're using fine-grained hardwood blocks, leave them unpainted or finish with varnish or oil before attaching the tapes.

3 Stand the blocks on end and, using a sharp pencil, mark a centerline for one tape that will go over, under, over, under all the blocks. Turn the blocks over and draw the same centering line on the opposite end.

4 Place the first block on a table. Attach a length of binding tape (available from any sewing shop) to one end of the block with two brads. The tape should be centered over the centerline. Then tack the two side tapes to the opposite end of the first block; set in each side tape 1⁄16 in. from the block's edges. Lay the tapes across the face of the block so the two side tapes go in the opposite direction to the center tape, as shown in the top drawing at right.

5 Place a second block on top of the first and wrap the tapes around the block (see the second drawing at right). Pull the tapes snug, but not too tight, making sure no tape is twisted. (If the tapes are too tight, the blocks won't flow when you operate the toy.) Tip the block on end and nail each tape with two brads.

6 Continue adding blocks and attaching tapes with two brads to the alternating ends of each block until you reach the top of the stack (see the bottom drawing at right). Trim the excess tape from the ends when the last block is in place.

If everything is done right, when you look at the ends of the blocks, you should see a pattern of single tape, double tape, single tape, and so on. Since there's no glue to dry, try the toy out right away.

JACOB'S LADDER

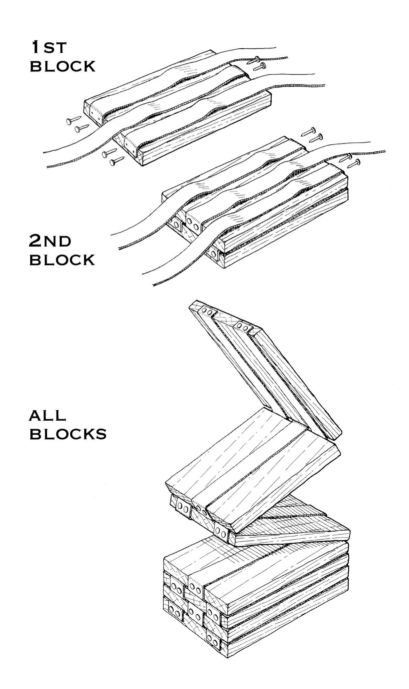

1ST BLOCK

2ND BLOCK

ALL BLOCKS

Flip the Acrobat

These little toys are truly ingenious and provide a lot of
laughs when they're passed
around. I've seen designs with a variety
of figures swinging about: monkeys,
clowns, acrobats, other animals of various stripes, and even one with Sigmund
Freud in his underwear!

The acrobat shown here costs virtually nothing to make and is surprisingly
rugged. The pivots for the arms and legs
are bent from paper-clip wire, while the
torso, arms, and legs were cut out from
plywood salvaged from a small clemen-
tine crate. The hardwood supports are
made from recycled pallet wood. Even
though "Flip" was built on a shoestring
budget, with a little practice you'll soon
discover that he's very sophisticated and
can make a lot of fancy moves. He'll flip
over the top and stop at either side, stop
at the top, split his legs over the string,
hold his arms straight out, and more.
The toymaker who first designed the
mechanism that flips the acrobat one
way and then the other on successive
hand squeezes (the secret's in the twists
in the tightly strung twine) must have
been some sort of natural genius. Why
didn't I think of that?

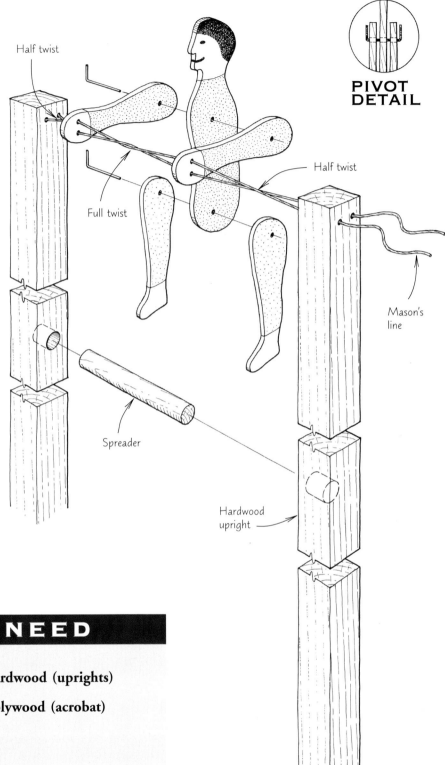

PIVOT
DETAIL

Half twist

Half twist

Full twist

Spreader

Mason's
line

Hardwood
upright

WHAT YOU NEED

- **2 pieces 12-in. x ½-in. x ½-in. hardwood (uprights)**

- **one 6-in. square of ¹⁄₁₆-in.-thick plywood (acrobat)**

- **1⁷⁄₈-in. x ¼-in. dowel (spreader)**

- **short length of mason's line**

- **small paper clips**

How to Make the Toy

1 Make the uprights from 12-in. lengths of ½-in. by ½-in. hardwood. Drill a ¼-in.-diameter, ¼-in.-deep hole for the spreader dowel about 5 in. up from the bottom of each upright.

2 Drill two ¹⁄₁₆-in.-diameter holes through the top end of each upright. Each hole should be set in ¹⁄₁₆ in. from the edge of the upright and ¼ in. from the top.

3 Transfer the pattern of the acrobat to a piece of ¹⁄₁₆-in.-thick plywood (or hardwood, if you prefer). Cut out two arms, two legs, and the torso.

4 Paint the figure as an acrobat, a clown, or whatever takes your fancy.

5 Drill ¹⁄₁₆-in.-diameter holes in the acrobat's arms, legs, and torso (as shown on the pattern on the facing page) and install pivot wires made from pieces of small-diameter, lightweight paper-clip wire. Bend the wire into a horseshoe shape (see the drawing on p. 111), with enough clearance so the limbs and torso clear each other with minimum friction.

6 Insert and glue the ¼-in.-diameter dowel in the holes in the uprights.

7 Thread mason's line through the holes in the uprights and the acrobat's hands, being careful to get the twists correct (see the drawing on p. 111). There are two configurations: a full twist between the acrobat's hands and a half-twist between each hand and the upright. Pull the mason's line so that when the twists are in and the line is snug, the uprights are parallel.

8 Knot the mason's line very tightly, and then melt the knot permanently closed with a soldering iron or with flame from a match.

FLIP THE ACROBAT

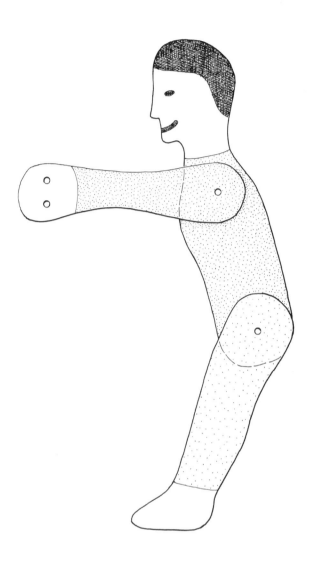

PATTERN

Scale

100%

Rocking Cradle

I studied a number of different cradle designs before building this rocking cradle and took the best from each: The design of the sides is from Massachusetts, the gently rounded headboard and footboard are from Maine, and the brace on the bottom is from Vermont. I decided to make the cradle from some sweet-smelling white cedar I'd had in the shop for some time, and when it was finished the design seemed so right and authentic the cradle just about jumped off the bench.

Some folk-doll cradles are very crude, some have squared off joints, some are handed down with the rockers broken off, and some have rockers just nailed on, split in rough use, and re-attached many times. I'm sure that all designs were treasured by their owners, but this little cradle embodies, I hope, the best of several folk designs and hundreds of years of accumulated play in its lines and construction. It should last for many generations.

Folk cradles were commonly made of $\frac{1}{2}$-in. hard pine, a wood now almost unknown. The cedar I used on my cradle is $\frac{5}{8}$ in. thick (a stock size for cedar) and seems just fine aesthetically, although the cradle is clearly robust. Half-inch plywood is, of course, available everywhere and serviceable; go ahead and use it if it's all that's available. Another option is to take $\frac{3}{4}$-in.-thick stock to a sawmill or cabinet shop and have it planed to $\frac{1}{2}$ in. Call first, and sometimes they can make it a part of a planing run at an economical rate. (You could get by with $\frac{3}{4}$-in. pine, maple, or birch, but it would be somewhat heavy looking.)

How to Make the Toy

I made this cradle to hold the rag doll featured on pp. 162-165. If your child has a good-sized doll, you may want to lengthen the cradle somewhat. If you want to use the cradle for toy storage, doubling its size will produce a significant volume of space for containing stuffed animals and other toys.

1 Enlarge the patterns on p. 117 and transfer to the wood. Cut out all parts with a combination of coping, crosscut, and rip saws. Be sure to make and install the rocker brace—it strengthens the rockers immeasurably.

2 Assemble all parts of the cradle with woodworker's glue and 2-in.-long brass flat-head screws. Drill pilot holes first and countersink the screw heads just below the wood's surface.

3 Round all the edges with 100-grit and then 180-grit sandpaper. Sand all flat surfaces smooth.

4 Finish with a light stain, satin varnish, or, if you're using cedar or a darker wood, a mixture of 50% linseed oil and 50% turpentine for an authentic look. Heat the linseed oil and turpentine to just below boiling point to encourage greater penetration of the finish. When the finish is dry, rub the wood with a soft cloth. Apply one coat a day for three days.

ROCKING CRADLE

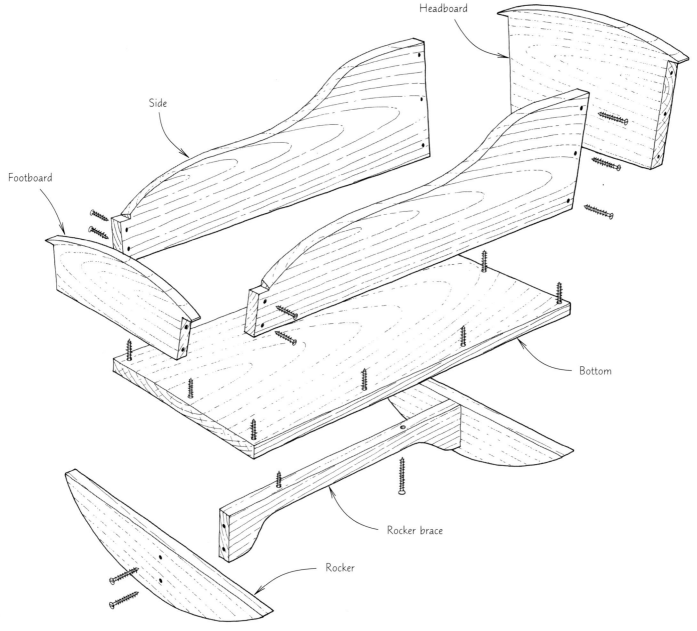

Headboard

Side

Footboard

Bottom

Rocker brace

Rocker

PATTERNS

Scale
37%

Enlarge
270%

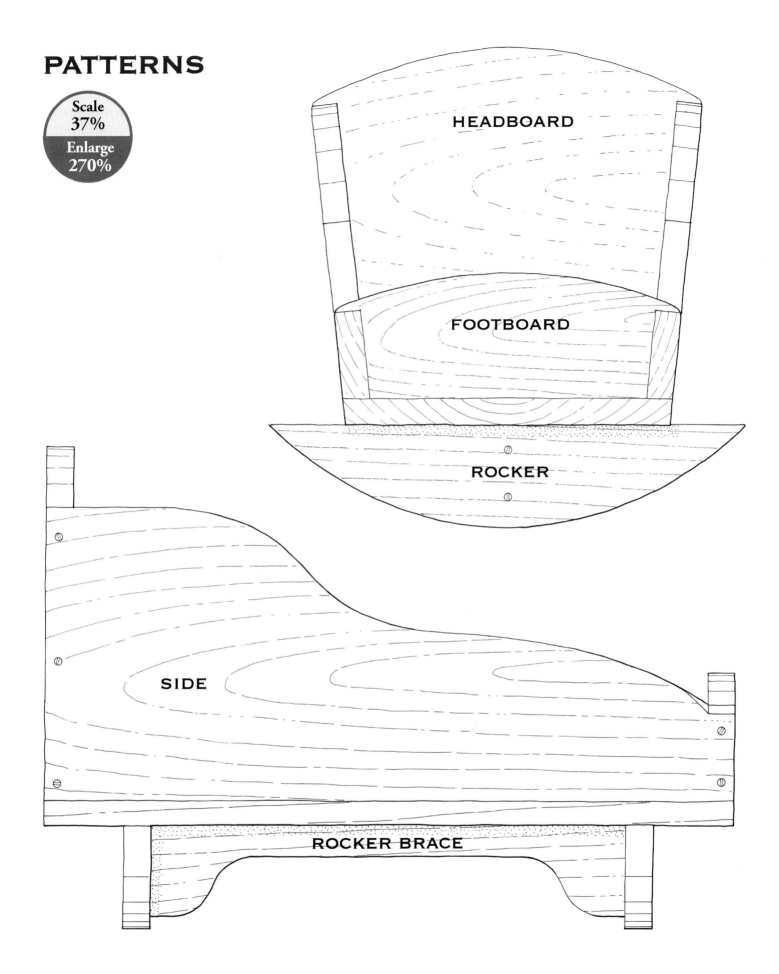

HEADBOARD

FOOTBOARD

ROCKER

SIDE

ROCKER BRACE

Herd of Elephants

Pull toys are surprisingly ancient, going back to Greek and Egyptian civilizations prior to 2,000 B.C. Many of the oldest surviving toys are made of clay, with turned wheels and stylized, beautifully wrought animals. (I'm sure that wooden pull toys were made too, but they haven't lasted.) The stroke of genius, of course, was the toymaker's decision to replace the toy animal's foot with a wheel, thereby making the animal mobile. And from a child's point of view, if an animal follows you around and stops and goes when you command, it must of course mean the animal has real affection for you.

Pull-toy animals come in many configurations, from single figures to herds (and even adults and their babies). Many of the animals move up and down, wag their tails, open and close their mouths, and so forth. These three elephants are a rather funny lot, going up and down in a rollicking series of movements as they are pulled forward on wheels with a cam action. Each of the body profiles is slightly different. The lead elephant has his trunk in the air and the trimmest waistline; the second has a slightly more rotund appearance, but still with his trunk up there, while the third elephant has his trunk down and a rather generous stomach. You'll find that kids really love this toy because of the way the elephant trunks and rear ends go up and down as the herd moves forward.

How to Make the Toy

1 Transfer the elephant pattern on p. 121 three times to ¾-in. plywood or hardwood, noting the varying stomach and trunk lines. Cut out the elephants with a coping saw or sabersaw. Fill any

imperfections in the plywood's laminations with quick-drying wood putty, and, when dry, sand all surfaces.

2 Drill holes for the dowel axles in the elephant feet with a ²⁵⁄₆₄-in.-diameter bit: This is ¹⁄₆₄ in. larger than the ⅜-in. dowel size. It's important that the hole size is not so big that the elephants flop about on their axles, yet not so small that the wheels bind.

3 Using a 2⅛-in.-diameter hole saw, cut out 10 wheels in 1-in. hard pine. (This thick pine is called "five quarter," or 5/4, and is available in any lumberyard.) Hold the drill and hole saw as perpendicular to the wood as possible while cutting the wheels (see p. 40). Six wheels (the front and back wheels) will act as cams, making the elephants go up

HERD OF ELEPHANTS

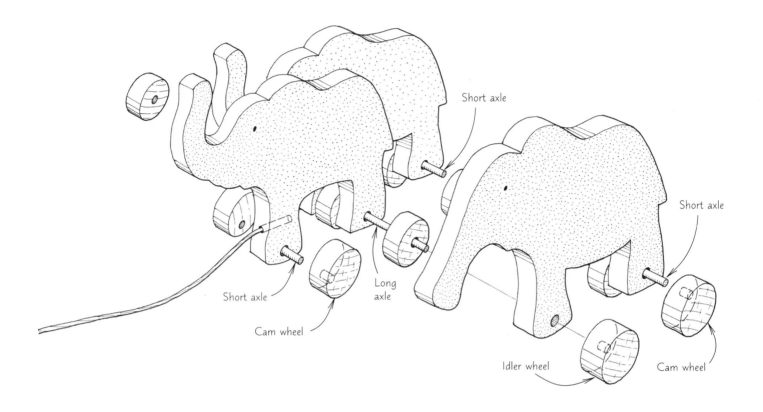

Short axle

Short axle

Short axle

Long axle

Cam wheel

Idler wheel

Cam wheel

and down, so fill their ¼-in. center holes with ¼-in.-diameter dowel. Glue, and then sand smooth.

4 Drill a ⅜-in.-diameter off-center hole in each of the six cam wheels. Set the center of this new hole ⅝ in. in from the circumference of the wheel and drill it ½ in. deep.

5 Paint the elephants (and the wheels, if you desire) before assembly.

6 Insert the three short axles through the elephants' feet, and then glue the three pairs of cam wheels on the axles. Use the glue sparingly so you don't smear any on the axle. Sight down each pair of wheels and line the two wheels up so they raise and lower the elephant at the same point in their rotation.

PATTERNS

Scale 65%

Enlarge 154%

7 The four wheels in the middle row are idler wheels (that is, they are not cammed). Drill out the center holes of the two inside wheels to $^{25}/_{64}$ in. diameter. Drill out the two outer-wheel centers to $^3/_8$ in. The wheels with $^{25}/_{64}$-in.-diameter centers will spin independently on the long dowel axle that joins the three elephants. Glue on the two outside idler wheels.

8 Drill a $^1/_8$-in.-diameter hole through the front leg of the lead elephant and attach a pull cord about 24 in. long.

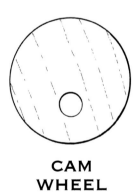

CAM WHEEL

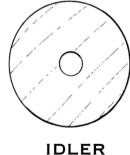

IDLER WHEEL

Carousel

Gravity-driven carousels with wind-up strings have been popular toys for generations, but with demand so much greater than supply they've become increasingly hard to find, even in antique stores. Precise details of the origins of toy carousels are vague, but the first miniature carousels apparently came to this country early in the 19th century from China aboard American clipper ships. Sailors brought them home to towns along the eastern seaboard, from where their clever design gradually spread inland.

This charming model combines the best points of several designs and has been a favorite of young girls for whom I've made a number of different versions. I am indebted to Mr. John A. Nelson (no relation) for this basic design, which I have enlarged slightly.

Just for fun, a while back I decided to make a miniature four-animal carousel using animal crackers that fit in little raised holders (as between small bookends) instead of wooden animals. There was only one problem: The children so regularly devoured every animal cracker, including the spares, that the carousel sat bereft of wildlife and suffered from neglect. But the children had a good time. If you downsize the present plan to make one for edible animals, be prepared to stock up!

How to Make the Toy

1 Use a compass to lay out three circles on ¾-in.-thick pine or high-quality ⅝-in. or ¾-in. plywood: Make two circles with a 3½-in. radius and the third with a 2½-in. radius. Push the center point of the compass ¹⁄₁₆ in. into the wood so you can find each circle's exact center when you drill the dowel holes later on.

2 Cut out the discs slightly oversized, and then bring them carefully to roundness with a broad file or lathe. It's especially important that the disc that supports the animals be as perfect a circle as possible.

3 Transfer the four animal patterns to scraps of pine or plywood with a hot iron (see the sidebar on p. 39). Cut out and sand the animals, using dowel files to get into the tight curves.

4 Cut out an ornament for the top of the center post. The ornament is traditionally the child's initial, a heart, or a ball; you can also use a large wooden bead (as I did), available from any craft store.

5 Drill ¼-in.-diameter holes through the animals to hold the posts, using a carpenter's awl to mark the holes and drilling pilot holes first.

CAROUSEL

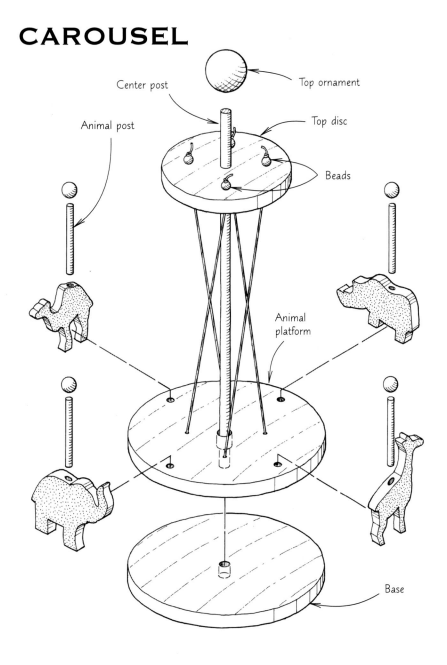

Center post · Top ornament · Animal post · Top disc · Beads · Animal platform · Base

6 Holding the drill at right angles to the workpiece, drill a 5⁄16-in.-diameter hole in the center of the base and top disc and a 7⁄16-in.-diameter hole in the animal platform. The extra 1⁄8 in. allows the platform to rotate freely about the 5⁄16-in.-diameter dowel.

7 Drill four 1⁄4-in.-diameter holes in the animal platform for the animal posts. Think of the platform as a clock face and drill the holes at 3, 6, 9, and 12 o'clock. The center of each hole should be set in 3⁄4 in. from the circumference of the disc.

8 Drill four 1⁄16-in.-diameter holes for the winding strings in the top disc and animal platform. Drill these two sets of holes with the discs centered over each other so the holes align perfectly. The holes are set in 3⁄4 in. on the top disc and should fall midway between the holes for the animal posts on the animal platform.

9 There are several ways to make the decorative balls on top of the animal posts. If you want to shape the balls from scratch, drill four 1⁄4-in.-diameter holes 1⁄4 in. deep in scraps of soft 3⁄4-in. pine. Glue in four 1⁄4-in.-diameter by 5-in.-long dowels and let dry: These dowels act as carving handles before they become posts. With a fine blade in your coping saw, cut out each pine piece into a 9⁄16-in. cube. Whittle and then sand into a ball shape. Alternatively, you can lathe-turn the balls from hardwood or simply use hardwood beads available from a craft shop as decorations.

10 Prime and then paint all parts with bright colors before assembling.

11 Glue the animals to the posts and then to the animal platform. Glue the

PATTERNS

Scale
65%
Enlarge
154%

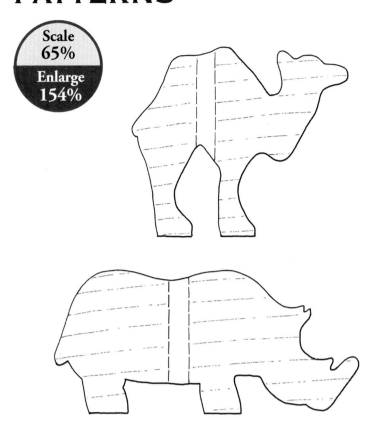

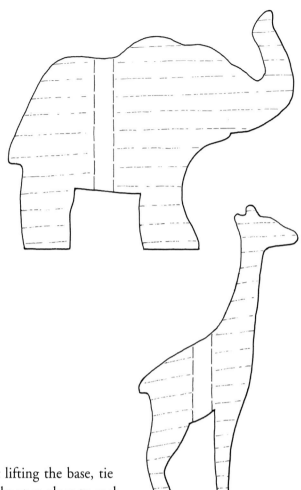

center post into the hole in the base and then slip the animal platform over the post, being careful not to get any glue between the platform and the post. Glue the top disc to the center post 2 in. down from the top of the dowel.

12 Cut four 12-in. lengths of nylon kite twine or mason's line for the winding strings (both materials wash clean better than common cotton string). Tie a double overhand knot in each string, melt the knot closed with a hot match, and then thread the strings from below through the 1/16-in. holes in the animal platform. Trim the knots carefully so they won't rub against the base.

13 Place four 3/16-in.-thick scraps of wood between the base and the animal platform so the platform rests perfectly parallel to the base. Thread the winding strings through the top disc and the small ornamental beads. With each

string snug but not lifting the base, tie a double overhand knot as close to each bead as possible. Remove the scraps of wood. If any of the winding strings is loose, simply raise it up and add another knot beneath the two already tied. When this operation is complete, each string should be of equal length and the animal platform should be parallel to the base. Melt the knots closed with a hot match.

The carousel is simple to operate. Lightly hold one of the animals and turn the topmost ornament as though you were winding a clock. The animals will all rise up as the strings become wound around the post in a pretty barber-pole pattern. Don't overwind— just let the strings come up snug against the center post. Then let go of the animal, and the carousel will turn back and forth many times, with the animal platform rising up and down.

Indian Ring Toss

I was pleasantly surprised to find this venerable folk toy in the athletic department of our local junior high school, where it is used, along with the game of Ping-Pong, to develop hand-eye coordination. The basic design of the ring-toss toy has its roots in the training of young Native American boys for spear fishing. The idea is to swing the rings up in front of you, and, anticipating when they will line up in a row, forming a sort of tube for a fraction of a second, spear through them to hit the fish.

It's harder than it looks. I must confess that I'd tried the ring toss about a hundred times without success. But recently one morning, still somnambulant before coffee, I picked up the toy and casually swung up the rings. Incredibly, they rose up before me in a perfect tube. I gave a mindless thrust with the dowel—straight through the rings, every one, and with no effort right into the beating heart of the fish!

How to Make the Toy

1 Use a compass to draw the inside and outside circumference of each ring on a piece of ½-in.-thick hardwood (or plywood if that's all you can find). The inside radius should measure ¾ in., and the outside 1¼ in. Lay out five, six, or seven rings (I've seen them in all three numbers).

2 Depending on the tools available, you can make the rings in one of two ways. If you have a lathe, first cut out the discs slightly oversized. Drill a ⅜-in.-diameter hole in the center of each disc, and then insert a ⅜-in. by 2-in. bolt with a large flat washer on each side. Tighten the nut securely and

WHAT YOU NEED

- 1 piece ½-in. hardwood, approx. 7 in. x 10 in. (rings)
- 4-in. square of ½-in. or ¾-in. hardwood (handle disc)
- 4-in. length of 1-in.-dia. dowel (handle)
- 8-in. length of ⅝-in.-dia. dowel (rod)
- scrap of 3/16-in. hardwood, approx. 2 in. x 4 in. (fish)
- 24-in. length of ⅛-in.-dia. braided nylon cord

mount the disc in the headstock chuck. True up the outside of the disc first, and then cut through the inside of the circle with a "parting" chisel.

If you don't have access to a lathe, saw around the larger (or outside) circle first, drill a ⅜-in.-diameter hole inside each circle, and then saw out the rings. (If you have 1½-in. and 2⅝-in. hole saws, you can use them to drill out the rings.) Sand the inside of the rings with a large dowel file and round over the outside circumference with a broad file.

3 Cut out or turn the 3½-in.-diameter handle disc from ½-in. or ¾-in. hardwood. Drill a ⅝-in.-diameter hole in the center.

4 Use a length of 1-in.-diameter dowel (or a piece of broomstick), approximately 4 in. long, for the handle. Drill a ⅝-in.-diameter hole 1 in. deep in one end to receive the dowel rod. Round over the opposite end of the dowel with broad files and sandpaper and drill a ⅛-in.-diameter hole through the end of the handle for the nylon cord.

5 Cut a ⅝-in.-diameter dowel 8 in. long, and then glue it into the hole in the handle. Round over the end of the dowel.

INDIAN RING TOSS

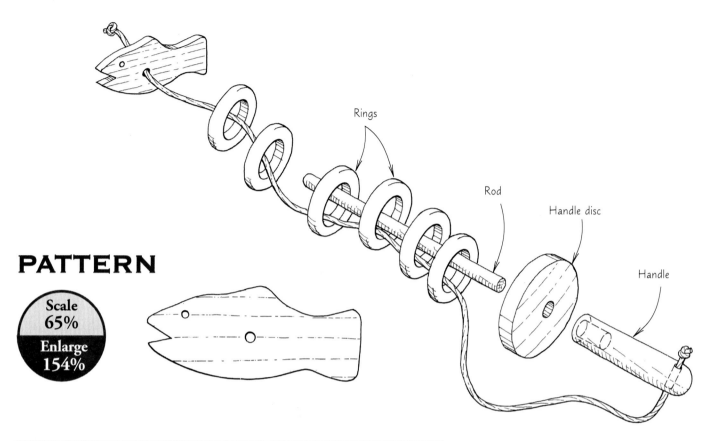

PATTERN

Scale 65%

Enlarge 154%

Rings

Rod

Handle disc

Handle

6 Slide the handle disc over the ⅝-in. dowel and glue the disc in place against the handle.

7 Transfer the fish pattern to a piece of ³⁄₁₆-in.-thick hardwood (or plywood). Cut out the fish and drill a ⅛-in.-diameter center hole for the cord and a ¹⁄₁₆-in. hole for the eye.

8 Paint the rings with three coats of any colors you like and finish the handle, rod, and fish with spar varnish.

9 Use about 24 in. of ⅛-in.-diameter braided nylon cord to join the handle and fish, securing both ends with simple overhand knots. Slip the rings over the fish, and give the toy a try!

Sailboat

No collection of toys worth its salt could possibly omit a miniature sailboat. Sailboats not only embody beauty and grace in motion but also possess a particular, almost inexpressible magic for painters, photographers, and children as well. And why not? There's a powerful mixture of congenial elements: the color and shape of the sails, the graceful curves of the hull, and the enchanting sight of the boat under sail, heeling gently to one side and pushed forward by the invisible hand of the wind. No wonder sailboats have for so long captured the imaginations of both children and the young in heart!

When I set about designing this toy sailboat, I knew I wanted a boat that was rugged, good-looking, and easy to build, but equally important was that it would perform well in the water—that is, be stable, hold a course, sail close to the wind, and go downwind. With these goals in mind, I dusted off the blueprints for a full-sized sailboat our family used to own, an Alberg 35, and combined elements of its hull shape, particularly the bow and keel sections, with "lift-based" construction, an ideal way to make a small hull.

"Lifts" are laminations of wood stacked parallel to the boat's deck. Lift-constructed hulls were used by boat designers in the days before computer simulations to demonstrate the complex geometry and calculus of boat design. The resulting models were constructed like a layer cake, with each layer a different shape or section from the deck on down to the base of the keel.

You might well ask by what logic you should go to the trouble of building the hull from five layers of ¾-in. pine rather than carving it from a solid block of soft pine. Here's why: A wooden toy sailboat has to be largely hollow, with weight at the bottom of the keel, if it is to sail properly. If you carve it from a solid block, the hull just weighs too much, and by the time you step the mast, attach the sails and booms, and add lead to the keel to keep the boat upright, the boat displaces so much weight that the decks are awash. The key to this sailboat's design is that the center portions of the top three layers, or lifts, are largely cut out to reduce the weight of the hull.

WHAT YOU NEED

- 1 piece ¾-in. pine, approx. 6 in. x 48 in. (lifts)

- 1 piece ³⁄₁₆-in. pine, approx. 1 in. x 3 in. (rudder)

- scrap of roofer's flashing lead (keel weight)

- 16¾-in. length of ⅜-in.-dia. dowel (mast)

- 8¼-in. length of ⁵⁄₁₆-in.-dia. dowel (main boom)

- 5-in. length of ¼-in.-dia. dowel (jib boom)

- 18-in. square of thin cotton or rip-stop nylon (sails)

- 2 small brass hinges

- screw eyes

- mason's line

How to Make the Toy

1 Transfer the five upper lift patterns shown on p. 133 onto a piece of ¾-in. pine, positioning the patterns so that no knots will show on the hull's surface. Cut out the lifts using a coping saw or sabersaw, and then cut away the center portions of the top three lifts as indicated on the pattern.

2 There are two ways to make the deck. If you are a purist, hollow out the bottom of the top lift with a sharp chisel until only about ⅛-in. thickness of wood remains. An easier method is to cut out all but ⁵⁄₁₆ in. in the width and length of the top lift, and then epoxy on a ⁵⁄₃₂-in. or ⅛-in. plywood deck (as shown in the drawing at right).

3 Glue all the lifts together (except the smallest, bottom one) with epoxy. When the epoxy has cured, sand the hull to shape with a coarse (60-grit) broad file and then successively finer grades of sandpaper. If you're like me, you'll be delighted by the lovely curvilinear shape that gradually appears as you sand away the excess wood.

4 Holding the drill perpendicular to the deck, drill a ⅜-in.-diameter hole for the mast.

5 The smallest, bottom lift is made from layers of roofer's flashing lead, which is available at any building-supply store. The hull pictured here used eight layers of lead flashing; you'll need to experiment with the keel's weight for your boat. Cut the lead with shears or a metal-cutting blade in a coping saw and attach it to the bottom of the hull with two screws. Sand to shape with a 60-grit broad file.

6 Cut out the rudder from a scrap of ³⁄₁₆-in.-thick pine and attach it to the hull with two small brass hinges, which allow you to move the rudder. You can use a utility knife to recess the hinges into the hull and rudder, but I found that it was easier to burn in the little "pockets" that hold the hinges with a small screwdriver. Heat the tip of the screwdriver until it is red hot, and then plunge it into the wood about ³⁄₁₆ in. deep. (Keep some water on hand in case the hull or rudder starts to smolder.)

SAILBOAT
HULL DETAIL

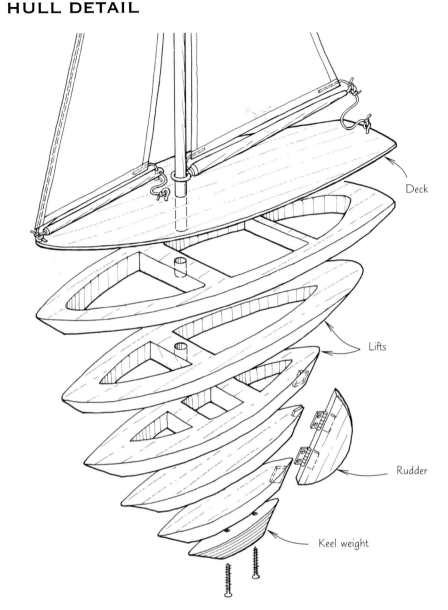

Deck

Lifts

Rudder

Keel weight

Before gluing in the hinges, make them a little stiffer-turning by tapping the pin assemblies with a small hammer —you want the rudder to turn, but with enough friction so that it stays where you put it. Epoxy the hinges in place.

(My basic boat has a simple steering system, but, if you want, you can add a little tiller and rudder post so you can turn the rudder from on deck. Make the rudder post out of a length of ¹⁄₁₆-in.-diameter brass rod, available from a plumbing-supply store or hardware store.)

SAILBOAT

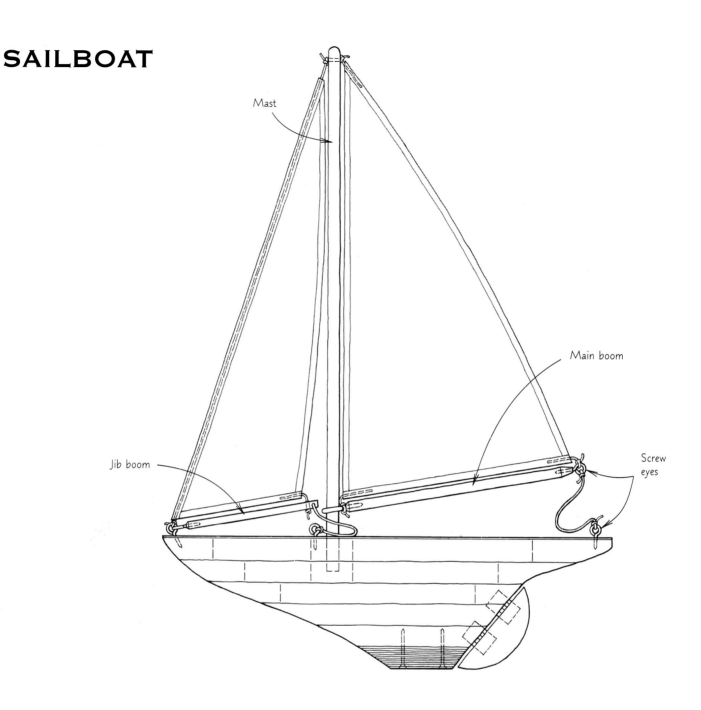

Mast

Jib boom

Main boom

Screw eyes

7 Paint the hull with your favorite color(s) and, if desired, stain and varnish the deck with two coats of spar varnish.

8 Cut the mast from a length of ⅜-in.-diameter dowel, the main boom from 5⁄16-in.-diameter dowel, and the jib boom from ¼-in.-diameter dowel. Taper the booms for appearance' sake, and then stain the mast and booms.

9 Make the sails from thin cotton or rip-stop nylon, available in most fabric

stores. You'll have to hem the cotton (as shown in the drawing above), but you can cut out the rip-stop nylon with a hot soldering iron, pressing the point down hard (it melts in a nonraveling cut). Melt the attachment holes in the rip-stop fabric with a 1⁄16-in.-diameter heated nail.

10 Assemble the mast, booms, and sails, using brass screw eyes and thin mason's line, as shown in the drawing above (see also the drawing on p. 131).

PATTERNS

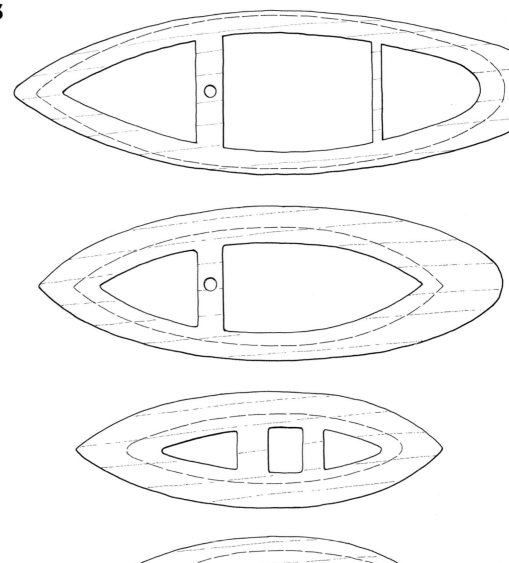

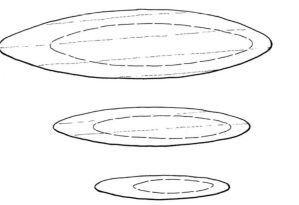

11 If you want a two-color paint scheme on the hull, float the sailboat in a tub of water and mark out the waterline with a pencil. When the hull is dry, paint the bottom below the waterline. Traditional colors are red, green, or blue.

Take the boat to a lake, pond, or pool, and note the wind direction. Pull the sails in to have the boat sail as close as 50° to the wind or let them well out to sail downwind. Have a child place the boat in the water and let it go! You may want to have a real boat on hand to chase it with.

This model boat sails even better at double the size shown here. Whichever size you make, the hull shape and boat are so pretty that your child may well want to keep the sailboat close by when it's out of the water. To keep the boat upright on a table or shelf, fashion a little three-piece cradle out of soft pine that conforms to the shape of the keel (see the photo on p. 130).

Jack-in-the-Box

According to the Oxford English Dictionary, the term "Jack-in-the-box," as it refers to the folk toy, entered the English language about 1702. But another definition of "Jack-in-the-box" appears much earlier, in 1542, "referring contemptuously to the consecrated host" and also to an early kind of burglar's tool, which enabled the user to force open safes and doors by dint of a small but powerful screw.

This elementary scholarship confirms my suspicions about old Jack: There is always something of the devil about him, something under-the-table and a bit wicked. Some scholars believe that Jack is related to Punch of the Punch-and-Judy shows because of historical references to "Punch-boxes," in which Punch, a grotesque and unsavory character with his hunchback and distorted face, popped out of a box to scare children. Punch-and-Judy shows go back to the late medieval and early Renaissance periods in western Europe.

This Jack-in-the-box is simple to make out of odds and ends of wood and other material. I've housed Jack in a very strong box, because it was always the box that finally fell apart when my children played with him.

How to Make the Toy

1 Cut a 4-in.-square bottom for the box out of ¾-in. pine. (The thick bottom is what gives the box its strength.)

2 Cut two 4½-in. by 4½-in. and two 4½-in. by 4-in. pieces of ¼-in. plywood for the sides.

3 Cut a 4½-in.-square top out of ¼-in. plywood.

- one 4-in. square of ¾-in. pine (box bottom)
- 2 pieces 4½-in. x 4½-in. x ¼-in. plywood (2 sides)
- 2 pieces 4½-in. x 4-in. x ¼-in. plywood (2 sides)
- one 4½-in. square of ¼-in. plywood (box top)
- small hardwood block (Jack's head)
- 48-in. length of large-diameter piano wire (spring)
- 2 small hinges
- 1 latch
- ¾-in.-long brads
- four ¾-in.-long round-head brass screws
- ¹⁄₁₆-in.-dia. bolts and nuts, or ½-in.-long brass escutcheon pins
- upholstery tacks, or staples
- scrap of lightweight cloth (Jack's cape)

4 Assemble the sides and bottom with glue and ¾-in.-long brads. Add four ¾-in.-long, #6-diameter round-head brass screws, drilling pilot holes in both pieces of plywood for each screw.

5 Attach hinges to the back side and the top with either ¹⁄₁₆-in.-diameter bolts and nuts or with ½-in.-long brass escutcheon pins bent over on the inside (use pliers to bend the pins). Attach a simple latch to the front of the box.

6 Make the spring from large-diameter treble piano wire, which is available from any piano tuner. To make the coil, wrap the piano wire around a 1-in.- to 1⅛-in.-diameter broomstick or dowel. Fix one end securely to the dowel with a couple of staples or a clamp. Wearing heavy gloves, start wrapping the wire closely together on the dowel. You'll want to make about 13 turns to get an actual 8-turn spring, because when you let go of the wire the spring will relax into a larger diameter with fewer coils. Bend the end of the wire with pliers to make a vertical piece about 2¼ in. long, and then make a hook in the top to hold on Jack's head. Cut off the remainder of the wire. The spring will seem a bit floppy, but don't worry.

JACK-IN-THE-BOX

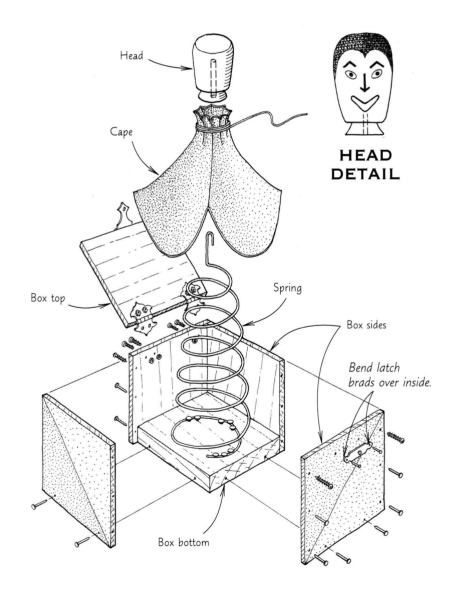

Head

Cape

Box top

Box sides

Spring

Bend latch brads over inside.

Box bottom

HEAD DETAIL

7 You can turn Jack's hardwood head on a lathe or simply carve one with a utility knife or jackknife and sand smooth. If you wish, make a nose from a short piece of dowel. Paint Jack's head as suits your fancy, giving an extra coat to the top of his head.

8 Paint the box with bright colors (geometrical shapes are traditional).

9 Attach the spring to the box bottom with about eight upholstery tacks or four staples. Bend and elongate the spring so that the top of the spring's hook protrudes about 2 in. above the top of the box.

10 Make Jack's cape from lightweight cloth (rip-stop nylon works well). Cut a small hole in the center, and place the cape over the spring. Trim the cape with scissors so it falls just below the inside bottom of the box. Set the cape aside.

11 Drill a hole in the bottom of Jack's head ¹⁄₃₂ in. smaller than the width of the hook and 1 in. deep. Line up the hole with the hook and press down on the head until the hook goes about ¾ in. into the head. Make sure Jack's face is facing forward.

12 Attach the cape to Jack's throat with three turns of twine. Glue the knot permanently closed.

13 Squeeze out enough sealant-type glue on the bottom of the cape to attach it to the bottom and lower sides of the box. While the glue is wet, move the cape to position the spring in the middle of the box so the head will not sag to one side. When the glue is dry, close the lid and try Jack out!

Spinning Top

Spinning tops, one of the oldest of all folk toys, date back to about 1200 B.C. in Greece and Egypt and to roughly the same time in China. Their long-term fascination for children seems nearly worldwide, and ancient examples abound from widely divergent cultures.

The top illustrated here is the best-running example of its size I've ever seen. The design is based on a top I found in southwest Texas; I've made a very small improvement in the handle design so that the top spins with a little less friction when you pull the cord. To make it easier for young children to thread the top with a pull cord, use a shoelace with a metal or plastic tip; putting a small handle on the pull cord makes it easier for children to pull it with authority.

Does this top ever go! If you put it on a smooth surface with a small lip (to keep the top from running off), such as those found on large inverted dinner plates or serving plates, it will run for 90 seconds, maybe longer.

WHAT YOU NEED

- 4½-in. square of ¾-in. hardwood (disc)
- 5-in. length of ⁷⁄₁₆-in.-dia. dowel
- 1 piece ¾-in. hardwood, approx. 6 in. x 2 in. (handle)
- 24-in.-long shoelace (pull cord)
- 2-in. length of ¼-in.-dia. dowel (pull-cord handle)

How to Make the Toy

You'll need a small lathe to make this top, but the toy is very easy to fashion and should take only 30 minutes or so of turning and sanding.

1 Cut out a 4¼-in. disc of ¾-in.-thick hardwood (maple, cherry, and beech all turn well on a lathe).

2 Mark the center of the disc with a carpenter's awl. Drill a ⁷⁄₁₆-in.-diameter hole through the center as perpendicular to the surface as possible.

3 Glue a 5-in.-long piece of ⁷⁄₁₆-in.-diameter dowel into the hole, so that 1½ in. protrudes from the bottom of the disc and 2¾ in. from the top. Twist the dowel in the hole to distribute the glue evenly. Let the glue dry.

4 Drill a ⅛-in.-diameter hole ⅛ in. deep in the middle of the short end of dowel. This hole is for the tailstock center of the lathe and keeps the dowel from splitting. Put a drop of oil in the hole.

5 Insert the long end of the dowel about 1 in. into the headstock's chuck and tighten firmly (but not so firmly that you crush the dowel). Put the tailstock's center into the hole in the end of the dowel and tighten moderately (too much pressure can split the dowel).

6 Turn the disc into a perfect circle using a gouge-shaped chisel. Using the same chisel and a small tool rest parallel to the disc, taper the disc top and bottom from a full ¾ in. at the center to ⅛ in. at the circumference. Any wobbling of the workpiece should now have been eliminated.

7 True up the disc with a straight-edged chisel.

8 While the workpiece is still in the lathe, sand with a 100-grit broad file or sanding block and then with 220-grit sandpaper. If you wish, add ornamental grooves in the surface of the disc with the corner of a chisel.

9 Using a straight-edged chisel, taper the short end of the dowel down to ⅛ in. at a point 1 in. below the bottom of the disc.

10 Paint or varnish the top while it is between centers. Making bright-colored bands on the disc is easy: Run the lathe at its lowest speed and apply color with a fine brush. Let dry.

11 Remove the top from the lathe and cut the short protruding dowel to 1 in. and the long dowel to 1⅝ in. Drill a ³⁄₃₂-in.-diameter hole in the long dowel ⅝ in. up from the top surface of the disc. Sand the dowel smooth with 220-grit paper.

12 Transfer the pattern of the handle onto a piece of ¾-in. hardwood and cut out. Drill a ½-in.-diameter hole through the handle to receive the top's upper dowel and a 1-in. hole in the side of the handle to allow pull-cord access to the hole in the dowel.

13 Make a small, 2-in.-long handle for pulling the cord from ¼-in.- or ⁵⁄₁₆-in.-diameter dowel. Drill a ³⁄₃₂-in.-diameter

SPINNING TOP

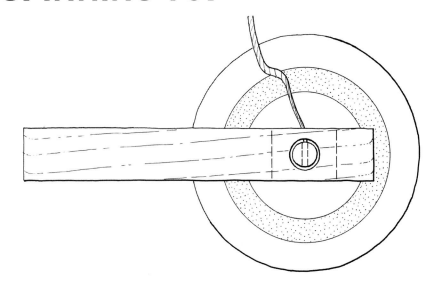

PATTERN

Scale
70%
Enlarge
143%

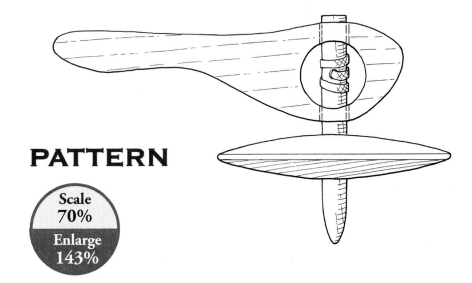

hole through the midpoint of the dowel. Thread the cord through the hole, and tie an overhand knot on either side of the dowel.

14 Place the handle's ½-in. hole over the top dowel, thread the cord through the dowel hole by reaching into the 1-in. hole, and wind by turning the disc. It doesn't matter which way the top spins. Give a lusty pull, and enjoy!

Tillie the Terpsichorean Queen

This humorous acrobat is one of many balancing folk toys collected by my colleague, Arnold Friedmann. Among his hundreds of examples, Tillie stands out for several reasons: She is agile, entertaining, and well balanced, and she is on the cusp between folk art and commercially produced toys. She has a lineage going back centuries in a tradition of balancing wooden toys, yet she looks forward to a commercial style reminiscent of Betty Boop, the comic-strip character. Tillie was actually patented in 1917 and sold, disassembled, in a little wooden box. She was manufactured by a company called The Toy Tinkers, which went on to design and sell the highly successful Tinker Toy, owned by nearly every boy (and many girls) I knew during the 1940s.

I'm not going to tell you what Terpsichorean means; as my mother used to say, you'll just have to look it up yourself.

How to Make the Toy

Tillie is an ideal project for the lathe, though if you have the patience you can whittle her torso to shape with a jack-knife. (I'd suggest using softwood if you plan to whittle Tillie.) You can also use wooden, craft-store beads for Tillie's head and feet and for the spherical stand parts if you don't have a lathe to turn them on.

TILLIE

1 Turn Tillie's torso on a lathe, using the drawing shown at right as a guide. The finished body is 1¾ in. in diameter at the widest point and 2½ in. long, so you'll want to start with a block about 2¼ in. square and 4½ in. long to allow for the spur and the tailstock center.

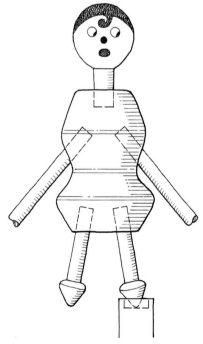

Since Tillie will be painted, any close-grained hardwood will do fine. You can save yourself vibration and wear and tear on the spur-center interface with the wood by planing ½ in. off the work-piece's corners (so it is eight-sided) before you put the block in the lathe. After turning the torso to shape, sand with 50-grit and 120-grit broad files and then 220-grit sandpaper.

2 Turn the feet and legs from a piece of ⅝-in.-diameter dowel, 2¾ in. long. Using a utility knife, carve the first 1 in. down to ⅜ in. diameter and set it in the chuck of the lathe. Tighten firmly, but be careful not to crush the wood. Because you are starting with a round surface, the wood turns easily with a sharp chisel. Next, smooth the legs and feet with the end of a broad file and a dowel file. The little balls of her feet are ⁹⁄₁₆ in. diameter. To smooth around the feet, use an emery board.

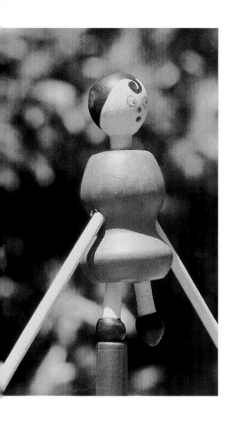

3 Gently taper Tillie's legs and feet with an emery board, making sure not to take off too much wood. (As diameters become small, the wood disappears at a surprising rate.) If in doubt, remove the legs from the chuck and finish by hand sanding.

4 To make Tillie's head, start with a 1½-in. cube of maple or other hardwood. Drill a ⅜-in.-diameter hole in the block and glue in a 3-in. long piece of ⅜-in. dowel. When dry, sand off the corners of the cube with a broad file, and then turn the cube to a ball shape 1³⁄₁₆ in. in diameter. Turn and sand the neck to ¼ in. diameter where it enters the torso. Cut the neck to length.

5 Drill a ¼-in.-diameter hole in the top of Tillie's torso, right on the vertical axis, and glue in the head and neck unit.

6 Make Tillie's arms from two 8-in. lengths of ⁵⁄₁₆-in.-diameter dowel. Drill a ⁵⁄₁₆-in.-diameter hole about ¼ in. deep into each round lead weight (the lead drills easily) and attach the dowel with epoxy.

7 Tillie's arms should come out of the body at 45° to her vertical axis. To drill the armholes in the body, it helps to use a 90° cardboard template as a guide. Divide the 90° angle into two 45° angles with a pencil line. Draw in the vertical axis on Tillie, then line up the line on the template with the axis; the cardboard will jut out at 45° angles on her left and right.

Mark the holes for the arms with a carpenter's awl, and then, using the template as a guide, slowly drill the ⁵⁄₁₆-in.-diameter holes. Dry-fit the arms in the holes. (If you completely misdrill one or both sides, don't worry. Just fill the hole with a scrap piece of dowel wet with glue, let it dry, cut it off neatly with a coping saw, sand, and try the hole again.)

8 Drill the holes for Tillie's legs in the same way, but be aware that the angle of the legs is much smaller (about 15°) than the angle of the arms. Glue in the legs.

9 Try balancing Tillie on anything that gives her arms room to clear the bench (a soda bottle with a concave cap will suffice.) She'll always balance in a more upright posture on one leg than the other. Because it is difficult to get her arms at precisely 45°, you may need to fine-tune her posture by either trimming one arm slightly or by discreetly sanding some lead off the weight that tilts lower.

STAND

The stand requires that you either turn three 1-in.-diameter and one 1½-in.-diameter hardwood balls on the lathe or see what you can scavenge or find in a craft shop ready made. The ball feet don't have to be exactly 1 in. diameter —⅞ in. or 1⅛ in. diameter would work fine—but they do have to match. The main engineering issue is that the vertical dowel has to be truly vertical, and it has to be high enough to provide clearance for Tillie's weights when she sways.

1 Cut three pieces of ⅜-in.-diameter dowel 5¼ in. long for the legs and one piece of ⅝-in.-diameter dowel 4⅜ in. long for the pedestal.

2 Drill a ⅝-in.-diameter hole ⅝-in. deep in the 1½-in. ball (the stand connector) to receive the pedestal. Dry-fit the pedestal to the ball (the dowel acts as a handle to aid in drilling the leg holes). Drill three ⅜-in.-diameter holes on the bottom of the ball for the three legs. Aim to make a tripod with each leg at the same angle.

TILLIE THE TERPSICHOREAN QUEEN

3 Glue the three ball feet to the legs, and then dry-fit the legs to the 1½-in. ball. Rotate the stand to see whether the pedestal is perpendicular. If it is not, carefully trim a little off the length of one or two legs until the pedestal dowel is straight up and down. When you are satisfied, glue all pieces.

4 Tillie's tiny dancing area at the top of the ⅝-in. dowel can't simply be drilled out, because it must have a flat bottom for her foot. Cut one end of a piece of ⅝-in. dowel at 90° in a miter box. Mark the center of the workpiece with an awl; then drill down ¼ in. with a ½-in. bit. Using a coping saw, cut off about 3/16 in. of the drilled-out section. If this new cut is not absolutely square, don't worry because you'll true it up later.

5 Sand the squared-off side of the little ring with 220-grit paper, and then glue the ring to the top of the pedestal (squared-off side down). Remove any excess glue from inside the ring with a cotton swab.

6 When the glue is dry, sand the ring down to 3/32 in. or so high. Try Tillie's foot in the little enclosure. You may want to sand the foot to more of a point if it rubs on the ring. When you have it right, Tillie should make a whole series of gyrations without stopping because of friction.

7 Paint the toy as you wish, but I would suggest that you keep the Toy Tinkers' design for her face: It's a classic.

(For those of you who can't wait to look up the meaning of Terpsichorean, Terpsichore was the Greek Muse of dancing and choral song.)

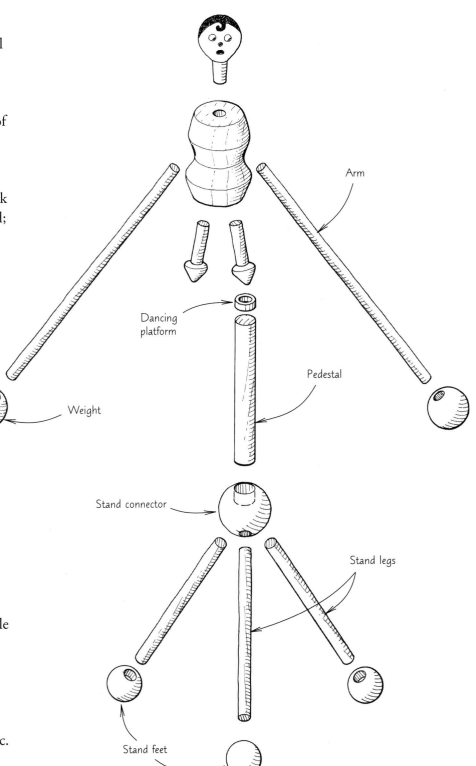

Arm

Dancing platform

Pedestal

Weight

Stand connector

Stand legs

Stand feet

Marble Game

I have a special affection for this marble game because it was the first folk toy I ever collected, over 25 years ago now. The original, a simplified, one-player version (shown in the photo on p. 20), was made by a local woodworker and mechanic named Cliff Ashley, of Cushman, Massachusetts, who, past 86 years old, fashioned the game from resawn, recycled pine. A tough Yankee if ever there was one, Mr. Ashley built it in a largely unheated shop with power from an ancient Fairbanks Morse one-cylinder gasoline engine and a pre–World War I bandsaw. When I asked him where he got the design, he replied, "Well, from my father. And I remember that he got it from my grandfather." Marble games have a pretty long pedigree.

My version of the marble game works best with two children racing marbles down the two sets of chutes; the chutes go in opposite directions, and the clearly visible marbles make a distinct "clack" whenever they transfer from one chute into another, so that you can hear which side is winning. The chutes are adjustable in pitch or "drop," so that by raising or lowering a couple of chutes, you can make the two sides run within a fraction of a second of each other, ensuring that neither child has an advantage based on choice of sides.

There's another way to have fun with this toy, too: Each child loads up one side, lets the marbles go, and then keeps cycling them as they come out the hole at the finish. With two busy children transferring marbles from bottom to top, the rhythms and syncopations of sound are a youngster's delight, and provide a chance for adults, if they so wish, to escape to a quieter room.

- **68 ft. of 1¼-in. x ³⁄₁₆-in. lattice (chute sides)**
- **34 ft. of ¾-in.-square pine (chute bottoms)**
- **6 pieces 25½-in. x 1¾-in. x ³⁄₁₆-in. lattice (6 uprights)**
- **2 pieces 8-in. x 3½-in. x ¾-in. pine (feet)**
- **2 pieces 21⅞-in. x 3-in. x ¾-in. pine (end pieces)**
- **1 piece 26⅝-in. x 3½-in. x ¾-in. pine (top piece)**
- **thirty-two #6, ¾-in.-long round-head brass screws and washers**
- **twenty-two 2¼-in.-long flat-head brass screws**
- **¾-in.-long headed brads**
- **marbles**

How to Make the Toy

Though it looks complicated, the double marble game is actually fairly simple (albeit somewhat time-consuming) to build. Essentially, it consists of two sets of eight chutes contained within a robust frame.

1 Make 16 chutes, 14 of them 24 in. long and 2 of them 25½ in. long, out of 1¼-in. by ³⁄₁₆-in. lattice sides and a ¾-in.-square pine bottom (see the cross-sectional drawing on p. 147). Sand all the parts before assembling, paying particular attention to the three inner surfaces of the chute. Use four ¾-in.-long headed brads and carpenter's glue to join each side of the chute to the bottom.

2 Using a framing square (or any accurate right angle), draw a "U" shape in pencil on your bench, with the uprights 24⅞ in. apart and 25½ in. long. Then

place one upright of 25½-in. by 1¾-in. by ³⁄₁₆-in. lattice along the inside of each vertical line, and tack to your bench with two small finish brads. These uprights are what hold the chutes in place.

3 Glue down one set of eight chutes to the two uprights so that each chute drops an equal amount. The top chute begins ¼ in. down from the top of the upright on the right side and drops to 1¼ in. down on the left side. (All measurements are from the inside of the lattice.) The top chute also begins flush against the outside of the right upright and stops approximately ⅞ in. from the outside of the left upright. This ⅞ in. of space allows the marble to drop to the next chute down, which is flush against the outside of the left lattice. And so they go, down to the bottom, with the marble-drop space alternating from side to side. The bottom chute is longer than the rest because it both catches the marble and transports it to the exit hole. Use just a tiny drop of glue on the last three chutes because you may wish to adjust them later.

4 Glue two 25½-in. by 1¾-in. by ³⁄₁₆-in. lattice pieces over the ends of the attached chutes so that they align exactly with the lattice tacked down to your bench. Again, use just a drop of glue on the bottom three chutes. Use weights or scrap pieces of wood to hold everything together until dry.

5 Build the second series of chutes over the first, beginning with the left upright and reversing each measurement as you go along. If there are any small variations in drop, replicate them in reverse on the second, or top, series of chutes. Again, save the longer chute for last and use just a little dab of glue on the bottom three chutes.

6 Place the final two pieces of 1¾-in. lattice over the left and right ends of the chutes, and attach with a drop of glue. Secure the uprights to the top five chutes with #6, ¾-in.-long round-head brass screws and washers.

7 When the glue is dry, gently pry up the side that is tacked to the bench (use a putty knife or thin screwdriver). Turn the assembly over and add #6, ¾-in.-long screws and washers to the side that faced down on your bench during construction. (Again, secure just the top five chutes.)

8 Cut out two feet from ¾-in. soft pine. You can make the feet in any shape you like (I used a half-moon pattern), as long as the bottom edge is straight and the foot is wide enough to provide stable support for the chute assembly. Hold the feet against the sides of the chute assembly and check to make sure that the game is perfectly vertical. Make any adjustments necessary, and then glue and screw the feet in place, making sure that the screws go into the ends of the chute bottoms. Drill a ⅞-in.-diameter exit hole for the marbles in each foot, lining the hole up with the chute.

9 Cut out the two end pieces and the top piece from ¾-in. pine. Take your time marking the screw holes for attaching the end pieces so the holes hit the center of the ¾-in. by ¾-in. section of the chutes that extend to the end (these are the "catching" chutes). Glue and screw the end pieces in place.

10 Drill a ⅞-in.-diameter entry hole for the marbles at both ends of the top piece. The hole should be centered 2 in. from the end of the top piece and ⅞ in.

MARBLE GAME

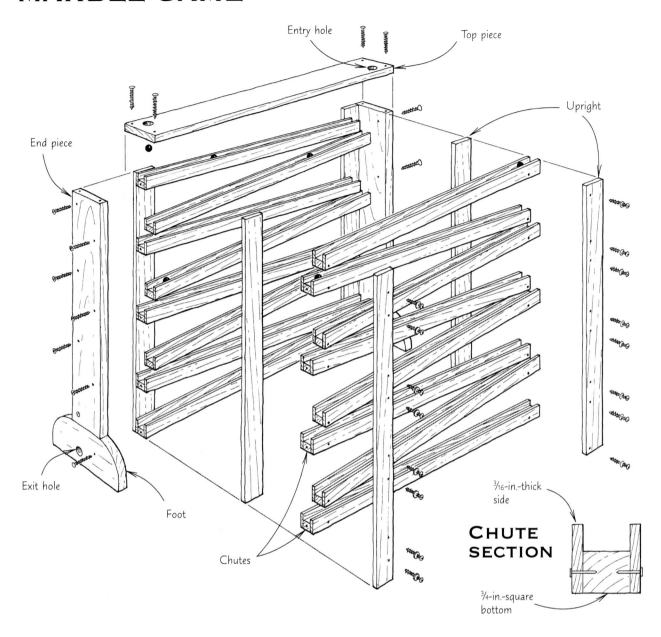

Entry hole

Top piece

Upright

End piece

Exit hole

Foot

Chutes

CHUTE
SECTION

³⁄₁₆-in.-thick
side

³⁄₄-in.-square
bottom

in from the side, so that when the marble is dropped into the hole it falls right into the center of the chute track.

11 When the game is complete, you may want to tune the chutes so that each side rolls with the same outcome (this is why you didn't screw down the three lower chutes earlier). To reposition a fast chute, insert a knife and separate the glue joint, and reset the chute at a

slightly shallower angle. Race two marbles again, and then switch the marbles to average out the elapsed times. When both sides run at the same speed, screw down the three bottom chutes from both sides.

12 Sand the frame with 120-grit sandpaper and then finish. Because there is so much pretty wood in this toy, I used varnish to show off the wood grain.

Self-Propelled Sled

I first came across the original for this sled up in Moosehead Lake, Maine, where an antique dealer had found it in a yard sale (see the photo on p. 15). I was so fascinated by the ingenuity of the sled that I asked permission to make working drawings from it then and there. A short time later, I made a replica in my shop and was yet more impressed by its 19th-century American combination of inventiveness and simplicity. It's a real working sled, from its sturdy seat down to its steel runners.

A child can work the dowel handle in a rowing motion and propel the sled across a flat patch of ground, or continue pumping down a slight gradient that won't allow gravity-powered sledding by itself. Then when reaching a real downward slope, the sledder just lifts up the crossbar (the "pusher") on the back of the sled, lets go of the propulsion mechanism, and steers with the feet. There are two steel pins on the pusher to help generate traction; for a heavier child, you could put in more. And there's a last bit of ingenuity: the two propulsion levers unfold in front of the sled to make a rather long pulling bar so that parents or older siblings can have the pleasure of pulling the child and the rig home after an afternoon's sledding.

How to Make the Toy

The sled is one of the more complex projects in this book, so I've broken the construction process down into two separate stages: first, building the sled and runners and, second, making the propulsion mechanism.

- 1 piece 11¼-in. x 11¼-in. x ¾-in. hard pine (seat)

- 1 piece 14-in. x 10-in. x ¾-in. hard pine (seat sides)

- 1 piece 8¾-in. x 5¾-in. x ¾-in. hard pine (seat brace)

- 1 piece 37-in. x 10¾-in. x ¾-in. hard pine (base)

- 2 pieces 22-in. x 4-in. x ¾-in. tongue-and-groove hardwood (2 back runners)

- 2 pieces 10¾-in. x 2-in. x ¾-in. hard pine (2 cross braces)

- 1 piece 10-in. x 2¼-in. x ¾-in. tongue-and-groove hardwood (front runner)

- 1 piece 18-in. x 3-in. x ¾-in. hardwood (steering bar)

- 1 piece 7⅝-in. x 2¼-in. x 1½-in. hard pine or spruce (lag-bolt support)

- 2 pieces 28-in. x 1½-in. x ¾-in. hardwood (2 short levers)

- 2 pieces 40-in. x 1½-in. x ¾-in. hardwood (2 long levers)

- 1 piece 15-in. x 2½-in. x ¾-in. hardwood (pusher)

- 11⅜-in. length of ¾-in.-dia. dowel (handle)

- 60-in. length of ¼-in.-dia. mild-steel rod (3 steel runners)

- 14-in. length of threaded rod

- twenty-six 2-in. drywall screws

- four 1¾-in. screws

- six 1-in. flat-head screws

- 6 steel 90° brackets

- one 5-in.-long x ⅜-in.-dia. lag bolt and washer

- six 2¾-in.-long x ¼-in.-dia. bolts

- two 2-in.-long x ⅜-in.-dia. bolts

SELF-PROPELLED SLED

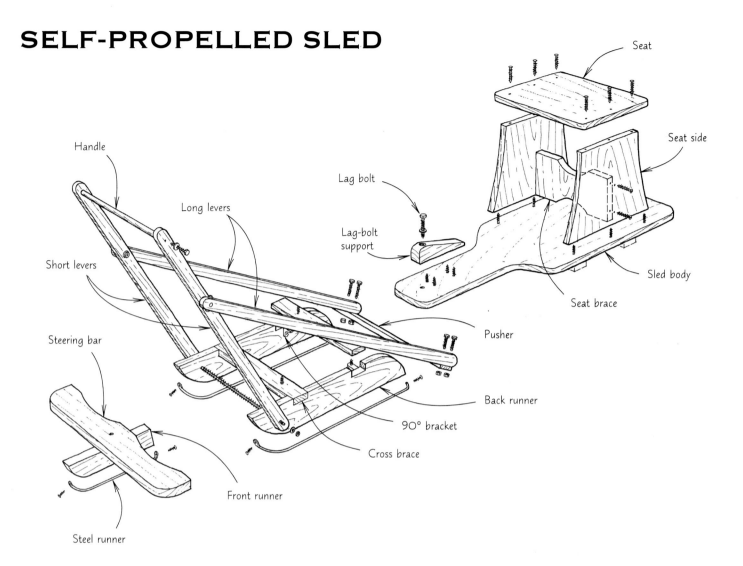

Handle

Long levers

Short levers

Steering bar

Steel runner

Front runner

Cross brace

90° bracket

Back runner

Pusher

Lag bolt

Lag-bolt support

Seat

Seat side

Seat brace

Sled body

SLED AND RUNNERS

1 Enlarge the patterns on p. 153 to scale up the sled body, seat, and runners.

2 Make the body of the sled from ¾-in. hard pine or hardwood. Cut out all the parts and attach the seat sides and seat brace, using a water-resistant glue and 2-in. screws. Then attach the seat top with glue and 2-in. screws.

3 Make the two back runners out of tongue-and-groove hard pine or hardwood. When you transfer the patterns, make sure the groove is pointing downward, because it holds the ¼-in. mildsteel runners. (The wood's tongue will be cut off.)

4 Cut out the two cross braces and attach them to the two back runners with glue and 2-in. screws.

5 Screw four steel 90° brackets to join the back runners and the cross braces.

6 Cut out the front runner from tongue-and-groove hard pine or hardwood and the steering bar from hard pine or hardwood and glue and screw together. Add the two 90° steel brackets that join the front runner and the steering bar (see the drawing on the facing page). These brackets are critically important because the front runner takes significant stress while the sled is turning while going downhill.

7 Using a hacksaw or a metal-cutting blade in your coping saw, cut the steel runners from a length of ¼-in.-diameter mild-steel rod (available at most hardware stores). Hammer a "flat" at each end of the three steel runners (six flats in all), making sure that the flats are in the same plane. To do this right, you'll need a minimum of a 16-oz. hammer and a large hard stone for an anvil. I used a glacial boulder of about 20 lb. and found it took 100 good whacks on the end of each rod to make a flat. It helps to hold the rod with a heavy glove. If all goes well, you'll have a "flat" thin and large enough to drill a hole in with an ⅛-in. bit.

Holding the rod in the groove of the runner and using your hammer judiciously, bend the rod to conform to the curve of the runner. Remove, and then overbend the rod ½ in. or so—or until it springs back to a shape that fits the runner exactly.

8 Attach the steel runners with ⅛-in.-diameter, 1-in.-long flat-head screws.

9 Cut out the lag-bolt support from a piece of 1½-in.-thick by 7⅞-in.-long by 2¼-in.-wide hard pine or spruce. Screw it onto the sled body with four 1¾-in. screws, driving the screws in from the underside. Drill a hole for a 5-in.-long, ⅜-in.-diameter lag bolt through the top of the lag-bolt support (set back 1½ in. from the front of the support), through the steering bar, and into the runner (see the drawing at right). Drill or chisel out a 1-in.-diameter recess ¼ in. deep for the 1-in.-diameter flat washer.

10 Screw the lag bolt with a washer under its head through the lag-bolt support and steering bar and into the runner.

11 Attach the back runners to the sled body with screws through the cross braces.

PROPULSION MECHANISM

The propulsion mechanism takes a lot of strain in kicking the sled along, so it must be constructed of hardwood. Oak, ash, hickory, and maple are good choices. The dimensions are not critical: If you find stock 1¾ in. wide or ⅞ in. thick, the levers will work just fine.

1 Cut two levers 28 in. long by 1½ in. wide by ¾ in. thick. Drill a ¼-in.-diameter hole about 1½ in. from the end of each lever for the lag bolts that hold the dowel handle.

2 From the same material, cut two levers 40 in. long. Drill a ⅜-in.-diameter pivot hole set back 1½ in. from the top end of each lever.

FRONT-RUNNER DETAIL

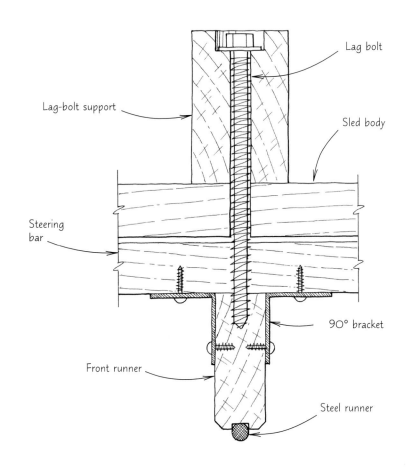

Lag bolt

Lag-bolt support

Sled body

Steering bar

90° bracket

Front runner

Steel runner

SELF-PROPELLED SLED
LEVER-CONNECTION DETAIL

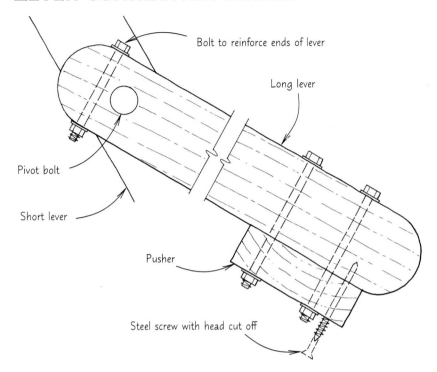

Bolt to reinforce ends of lever

Long lever

Pivot bolt

Short lever

Pusher

Steel screw with head cut off

9 Measure the threaded rod so it protrudes 1¼ in. from the outside of the runners. Cut to size.

10 Attach the short levers to the threaded rod, with a flat washer between the lever and the runner and a flat washer and an acorn nut finishing off each end of the rod.

11 Pull the short levers all the way forward, so they rest on the steering mechanism. Place the long levers and the pusher on the sled body so that the full width of the pusher sits at the end of the sled.

12 Mark each short lever for a hole that allows a ⅜-in. bolt to pass through both sets of levers. (You've already made the ⅜-in. hole in each long lever.)

13 The ends of the long levers are subject to a lot of strain. Reinforce them by inserting a ³⁄₁₆-in.-diameter by 1¾-in.-long bolt through the width at the end of each lever (see the drawing at left).

14 Insert two or more steel pins made from 1¾-in. screws with their heads cut off in the back of the pusher. Drill pilot holes and thread the screws in with pliers.

15 Disassemble the levers, and then sand and paint the entire sled. I kept the Christmas color scheme of the original sled for my replica: All the levers, the sled body, the seat sides and seat brace, and the front runner are painted a bright red; the handle, the seat top, the edges of the seat sides, and the lag-bolt support are a gloss green. The only parts I didn't paint are the steering bar and two rear runners, which I gave three coats of spar varnish.

Before you go sledding, coat the bottom of the metal runners with candle wax. The sled runs best on packed or icy snow.

3 Cut out the "pusher" from a piece of ¾-in. hardwood.

4 Drill two ¼-in.-diameter holes through the width of each long lever (at the bottom end) for attaching the pusher. Secure the pusher to the levers with ¼-in.-diameter, 2¾-in.-long bolts, nuts, and washers.

5 Drill ¼-in.-diameter holes for the threaded rod in the short levers.

6 Cut a piece of ¾-in.-diameter dowel or broom handle 11⅜ in. long for the sled handle.

7 Drill a ³⁄₁₆-in.-diameter hole in the center of each end of the handle, and attach the 28-in. levers to the handle with ¼-in. by 2¾-in. hex-head lag bolts and washers.

8 Mark the ¼-in.-diameter hole for the threaded rod on the back runners. Drill a hole in both runners.

PATTERNS

Scale
20%
Enlarge
500%

STEERING BAR

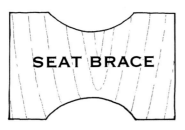

SEAT BRACE

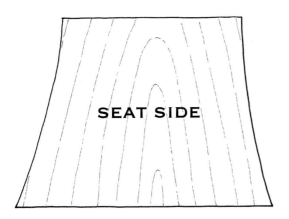

SEAT SIDE

FRONT RUNNER

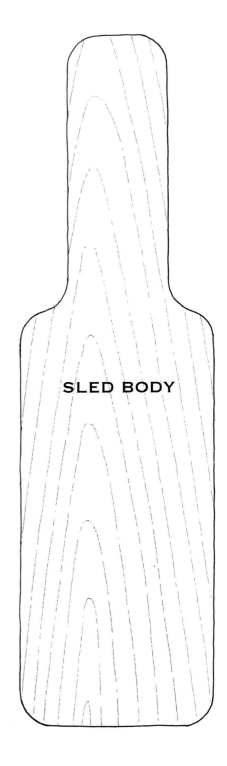

SLED BODY

BACK RUNNER (x 2)

Saltbox Dollhouse

Dollhouse designs typically fall into one of two categories: (a) super-complicated bric-a-brac, kit-form, or finished Victorian houses designed more for parents than children, or (b) unimaginative boxes all but bereft of significance or personality. Ah, but there is a third class of dollhouse—the historically interesting design that is, nevertheless, simple and strong. The basic replica of a New England saltbox shown here exemplifies the latter, and its lines are pleasantly familiar to anyone interested in indigenous American architecture of the 17th and 18th centuries.

Saltbox houses were designed for the cold New England climate, where prevailing winds robbed houses of heat. (January winds still steal heat, but 250 years ago, before central heating, insulation, storm windows, or Franklin's invention of the box stove, keeping much above 40°F was doing well.) The saltbox house with its two stories facing away from the wind and its roof line on the other side sometimes descending almost to the ground lifted the frigid wind up over the house, and thus prevented the direct assault of cold wind on a flat, vertical surface.

The saltbox was a house that often evolved. At first, the family would build just what we have in this dollhouse: two large rooms, including a kitchen area, on the first floor and sleeping quarters on the second. When there was enough money, the family would enlarge the house. By moving the kitchen out into the back, in a single story, and then continuing the roof line almost to the ground, they also created a lean-to woodshed right next to the kitchen, and a roof line so distinctive that it generated its own homely name, the "salt box."

The saltbox dollhouse depicted here can be built on several levels of complexity. In its simplest form, you can

WHAT YOU NEED

- **1 piece 32-in. x 14¼-in. x ⅝-in. or ¾-in. plywood (base)**
- **1 piece 8-ft. x 4-ft. x ¼-in. shop-grade birch plywood (roofs, walls, floors, dormers, door)**
- **8-ft. length of ⅜-in. x 3/16-in. pine (ceiling molding)**
- **4-ft. length of 3/16-in. x ⅛-in. pine (chair-rail molding)**
- **13-ft. length of ½-in. x ⅛-in. pine (baseboard molding)**
- **21-ft. length of ¾-in. x ⅛-in. pine (exterior trim molding)**
- **two small brass hinges**
- **thin stock for optional window mullions, stairs**

leave out the dormers, just as people did when starting out in the 17th century. (It was called "gettin' th' place tight to the wetha.") And you can leave out the little staircase, replacing it with a simple partition wall to hold up the second floor. This will produce a very serviceable toy that a child will love. Then when you have more time, you can add the dormers, staircases, and other details.

The staircase is a sort of prop for the imagination, and can be made very prettily with small strips of oak for the stair treads. The whole staircase unit can be constructed outside the house, inserted from the back, and then glued in place. Dormers transform the second story inside—the sloped ceiling cutouts give the saltbox dollhouse the unmistakable look of another era. If you want to be historically accurate, design in a 2¾-in.-square by 22-in.-high softwood central chimney (but install it before assembling the house). Saltbox houses were originally heated by numerous fireplaces, all

SALTBOX DOLLHOUSE

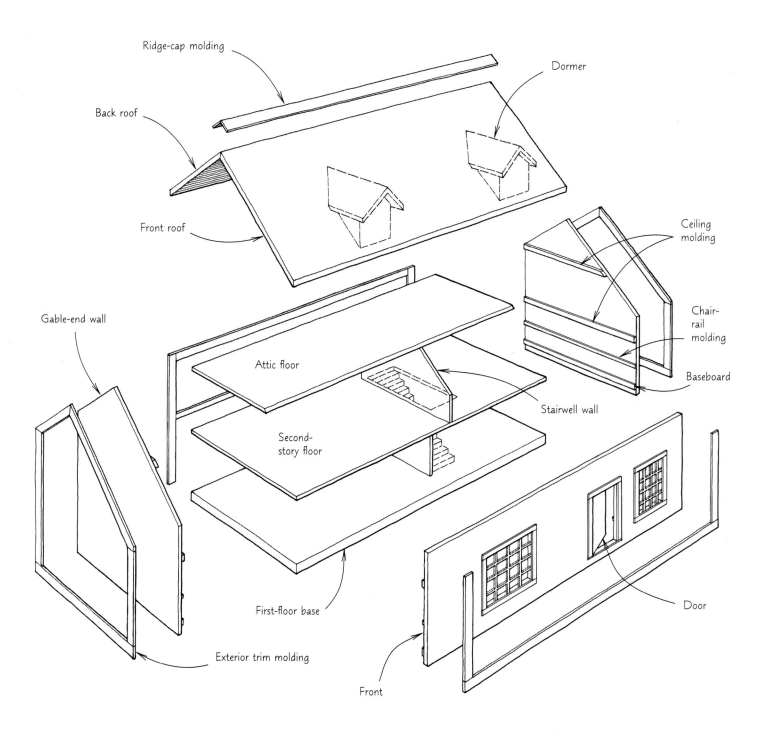

Ridge-cap molding

Dormer

Back roof

Front roof

Ceiling molding

Gable-end wall

Chair-rail molding

Attic floor

Baseboard

Stairwell wall

Second-story floor

First-floor base

Door

Exterior trim molding

Front

venting into the central masonry, and in the model you could chisel out little fireplaces in the chimney on each floor before assembly.

Lastly, historical accuracy and suggestiveness know few bounds in dollhouses, and with your child or grandchild, you can glue on false, stained ceiling joists after the ceiling is painted. Or, if you're a glutton for punishment, you could make a jig and saw out clapboards from soft pine, or shingle the house, as was common on the seacoast.

There are all manner of things to do cooperatively with a child to personalize a dollhouse. Leftover scraps of wallpaper and spray-on adhesive transform a room (easiest done before assembly—after assembly use real wallpaper paste); simple furniture made from 1/8-in.-diameter dowel legs and 1/8-in.- to 1/4-in.-thick plywood can be moved about; lighting with little penlights or miniature Christmas-tree bulbs is brilliantly evocative at night; or try cotton snow and a little sleigh on the roof for the holidays. Each year, you might want to make a small project together.

How to Make the Toy

Making the basic dollhouse is straightforward. Like the Jack-in-the-box on pp. 134-136, the key to its strength is the 5/8-in.- or 3/4-in.-thick plywood base. Outer walls are glued and nailed to the floor, and inner partitions are glued to it, too. The plywood is rigid enough to provide a torsion-free base for the whole house. All other large surfaces—roofs, floors, and exterior and interior walls—are made from 1/4-in. shop-grade birch plywood (which is high quality on both sides).

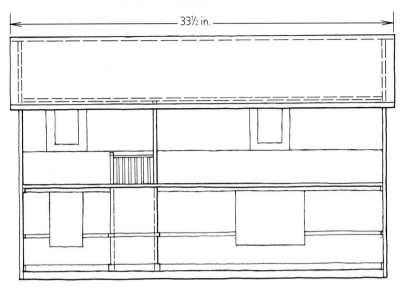

BACK ELEVATION

33 1/2 in.

FRONT ELEVATION

32 in.

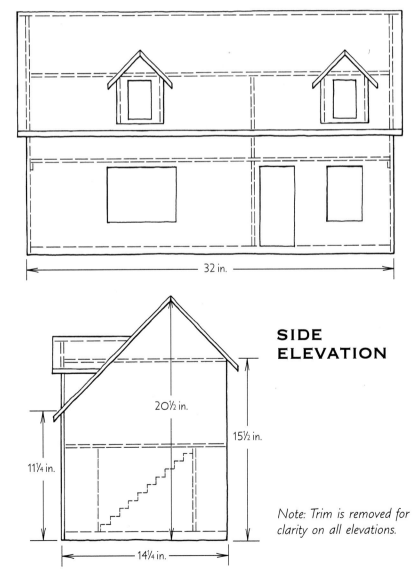

SIDE ELEVATION

20 1/2 in.

15 1/2 in.

11 1/4 in.

14 1/4 in.

Note: Trim is removed for clarity on all elevations.

1 Cut out the base of the dollhouse from a piece of ⅝-in.- or ¾-in.-thick plywood. The base measures 32 in. by 14¼ in.

2 Lay out all the structural parts of the dollhouse on a 4-ft. by 8-ft. sheet of ¼-in.-thick shop-grade birch plywood, leaving enough space between the parts to allow cutting with a sabersaw or crosscut saw. You'll need the following parts: house front (32 in. by 11 in.); second-story floor (31½ in. by 14 in.); attic floor (31½ in. by 10 in.); two gable-end walls (14 in. wide by 20⅛ in. at the peak); front roof (33½ in. by 14¾ in.); and back roof (33½ in. by 8¾ in.).

If you plan to build the two dormers, you'll also need to lay out their front, sides, and roofs on the ¼-in. plywood (see the drawing on p. 160). If your house will have stairs, you'll need to lay out the walls for the stairwell (see the drawing on the facing page); if you don't want to build stairs, lay out one or two interior partitions.

3 Cut out all the parts, including the openings for the windows and door. If you choose to make the dormers, cut out the holes in the roof for the dormers now. Cut the dormer roofs a little oversized in length (see p. 161). To avoid splintering the thin plywood, use a fine-toothed crosscut saw or a sharp, fine-toothed, high-quality blade in a sabersaw.

4 It's a lot easier to do all the interior detailing to the house (moldings, window trim, etc.) while the walls, floors, and roofs are disassembled. Using glue and short brads, attach the ceiling molding (which holds up the second-story floor) to the inside of the front wall and two gable-end walls. The top of the molding should be 7½ in. up from the bottom edge of the walls. Attach the chair-rail moldings with epoxy or yellow carpenter's glue. Use spring-close clothespins as small clamps. Dry-fit the sides and front of the house and trim where necessary.

5 Windows can be made on several levels of detail. On the simplest level, you can simply leave the openings in the plywood and dress them up with trim molding around the window opening. Alternatively, you can glue thin pieces of Plexiglas on from the inside, with or without window panes painted on. The prettiest route (but also the most time-consuming) is to make lattice-like mullions out of thin-cut pieces of interlocking hardwood (see the drawing on p. 160). Notch the mullions with a utility knife.

6 Attach the front door with small brass hinges or glued-down pieces of supple leather.

7 To make crisp paint demarcations between parts, it's best to paint all interior surfaces before assembly. The choice of colors is up to you, of course, but white is traditional for the ceilings, and contrasting colors above and below the chair rails look particularly attractive (see the photo on the facing page). You might also consider staining the floors rather than painting them, since birch plywood stains beautifully and seals well with two coats of varnish. Staining a whole room

STAIRCASE

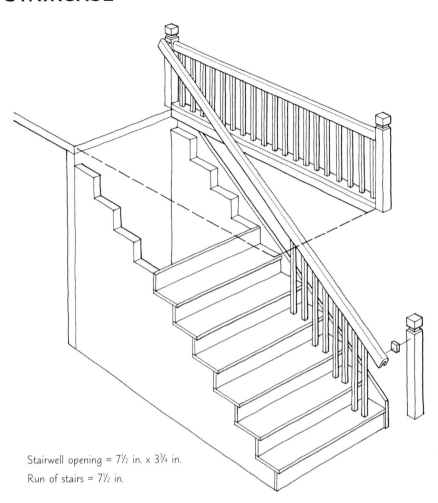

Stairwell opening = 7½ in. x 3¾ in.
Run of stairs = 7½ in.

with a light stain also looks wonderful. Wait to paint the outside surfaces until after assembly.

8 When the interior detailing is finished to your satisfaction, assemble the plywood base and the three exterior walls. You can hammer brads directly through the ¼-in. plywood into the ⅝-in. or ¾-in. plywood base (spread glue first), but drill pilot holes where ¼-in. plywood nails into the end grain of ¼-in. plywood. Wipe off any excess glue.

9 Dry-fit the second-story floor. If you decide to make the stairway, remember to cut out the opening in the second floor. Don't glue in this floor until everything beneath it is the way you

SALTBOX DOLLHOUSE

DORMER

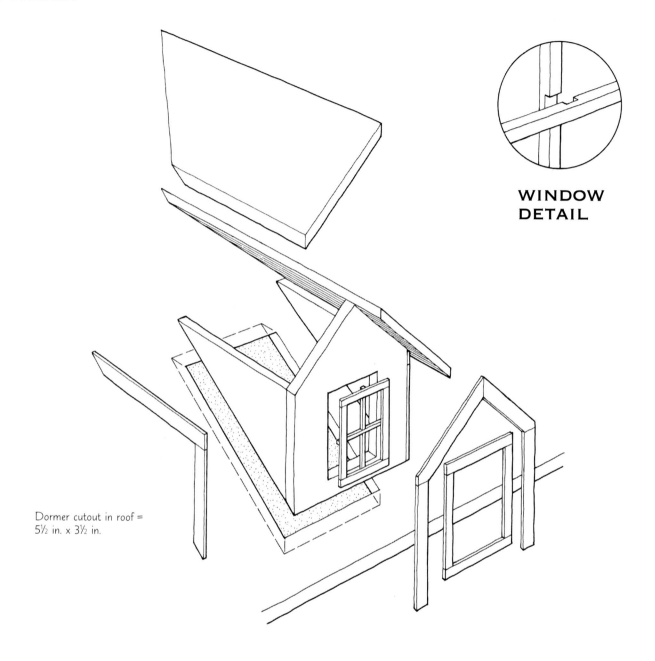

WINDOW DETAIL

Dormer cutout in roof =
5½ in. x 3½ in.

want it! Once the floor is permanently in place, it greatly limits access. If you've built a stairway, glue it in position now.

10 The attic floor/second-story ceiling is not absolutely necessary, but it does add strength and authenticity to the house. As with the second-story floor, don't glue it in place until the room below it is as you like it.

11 If you're not installing a stairway in your house, glue in an interior wall cut from the ¼-in. plywood between the first and second floor. You can also add a partition between the second floor and attic floor. Add other details (baseboard, ceiling, and chair-rail molding) as desired.

12 If you decide to attach dormers at this stage of the dollhouse's evolution, it's easier to do so before you attach the main roof. Build the dormers out of ¼-in. plywood, using the drawing on the facing page as a guide.

The dormer roofs join the main roof at a compound angle, which is quite tricky to cut. But because the plywood is so thin, you can use a coarse-grit broad file to sand the compound angle without having to get involved in any complex roof-angle geometry. Cut the roof pieces a little long where they intersect with the main roof. Glue and nail together the dormer on the bench, with the roof pieces extending backward an extra ⅛ in. or ³⁄₁₆ in. Then attach a piece of 50-grit paper to the roof with dabs of sealant-type glue. When the glue on the dormer is dry, pick up the whole unit in your hand, and sand it into the contour you want right on the roof. Everything is facilitated by the fact that the roof is at a 45° angle to perpendicular.

13 The two sides of the roof come together at a 90° angle, so that each roof plane is at 45° to perpendicular. Assemble the two sides on the bench. If the roof's ridge is difficult to line up smoothly, position it a little "proud" or oversize, and sand with a broad file. If you wish, hinge the rear roof at the peak for access to the attic.

14 Attach the roof to the sides of the house with glue and brads. If you haven't decided on the dormer question yet, you can screw on the roof with countersunk ¾-in.-long by #6 flat-head screws so you can remove it later on.

15 Sand all exterior surfaces with 220-grit sandpaper.

16 Paint the roof and the exterior of the house. The roof looks good a light gray (to imitate slate), and the house can be any color—barn red, white, weathered cedar shingle, and weathered siding are traditional. If the exterior of the house is all one color, attach the exterior trim boards and house corners first (with glue and brads). Cut the boards a little long, and mark with a sharp pencil right on the house; then fit to size with a coping saw. With the trim installed, paint the whole house. If the trim boards contrast in color with the house (as on the dollhouse shown here), it's a lot easier to paint the boards first before you install them.

17 Glue four small scraps of rug or other material to the bottom of the dollhouse so it doesn't scratch the floor or table.

Rag Doll

Dolls are among the oldest, most loved, and most collected of all toys. In 18th-century America, most home-crafted dolls were either carved of wood or sewn from cloth; then, after about 1825, came rope dolls, with rope arms and legs. Combinations of cloth and wood were also popular, with wooden heads and cloth bodies being the most prevalent, but sometimes, as with the wonderful Bangwell Putt doll (see p. 10), carved hands also appeared. Rag dolls are a perfect example of folk art, where available talent in a family and accessible raw materials at little or no cost defined much of the medium.

The cloth doll pictured here was sewn by my wife, Rennie, after looking at many such dolls; the face is based on a rag doll from around 1900, which in itself is probably a drawing based on expensive porcelain dolls of the era. Many drawn faces from the 1880s and earlier were very severe and would probably scare the socks off little girls today.

How to Make the Toy

1 Cut out a 24-in. square of medium-heavy, untreated cotton cloth.

2 Because the doll is likely to receive a lot of handling, it's a good idea to dye the white cotton cloth a darker color. You can use a commercial dye, but this old folk recipe is more effective and produces a surprisingly antique look: Mix 2 quarts of hot water, about 1½ cups of strong tea, and a cup of salt to "set" the dye. Soak the cloth in the mixture for eight hours or overnight, stirring occasionally to distribute the dye evenly.

3 Check the color of the cloth. If you want a darker shade, let the cloth soak longer. (Be aware that when you rinse the cloth, it will lighten slightly. After rinsing, you can always pop it back in the dye.)

4 Rinse, dry, and then iron the cloth. Transfer the pattern on p. 164 to the cloth twice to make the front and back.

5 Sew the two halves together with the smoother sides of the cloth pieces facing each other and the "wrong sides" out. Stitch with a sewing machine or by hand, leaving a 4-in. gap below one arm, down to the hip. If you wish, you can double-sew all seams for strength.

6 Turn the doll right-side out by pulling it through the 4-in. hole.

7 Stuff the doll with tiny scraps of soft cloth or socks (the traditional way) or, for a smoother doll, with polyester quilt batting, which is available at sewing and crafts shops. Work the fill down into the doll's arms and feet with your fingers. Work the fill about inside the head to get the face as smooth as possible, and finish by stuffing the torso. Sew up the 4-in. hole by hand.

RAG DOLL

PATTERN

Scale 50%

Enlarge 200%

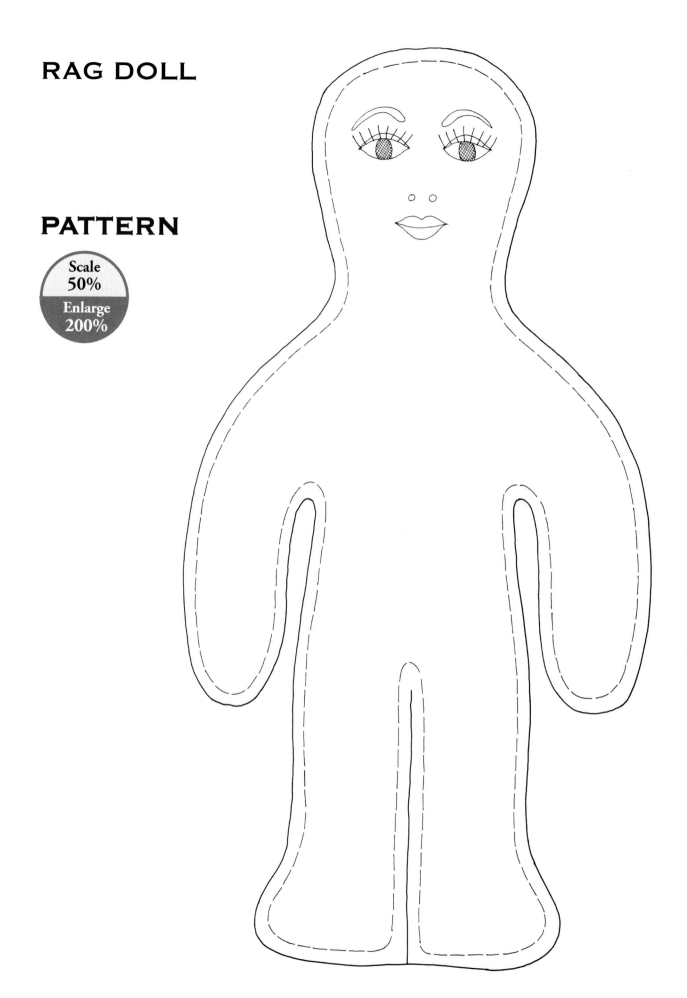

HAIR DETAIL

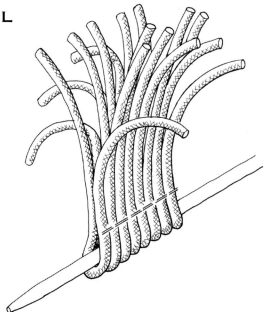

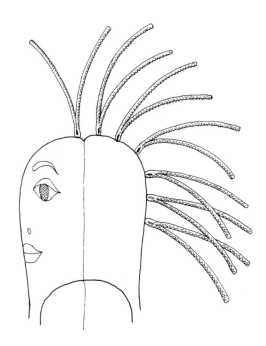

8 Lightly draw in the face with a pencil.

9 Make the doll's hair from strands of heavyweight wool yarn cut 10 in. long. Take enough strands to make a row 3 in. wide and place them flat on a table. Fold the strands over a knitting needle placed across the middle, or at the 5-in. mark. You now have a "unit" of doll hair (some might call it an implant). Sew across the unit just below the knitting needle. Make about 30 units for a thick head of hair.

10 Divide the units of hair into three equal bundles—one for the back of the head and one for each side. Starting at the back of the head, about halfway down, sew on successive units toward the top of the head, stopping at the seam line. The starting point will determine the overall length of the hair and will depend on the number of units you have made (the lower the starting point, the more units needed). Work in the same way on each side, joining the units at the back of the head and bringing each around to the seam line at the front.

11 When the hair is sewn in, draw in permanently the details of the face to integrate them with the hairline. Color the lips and eyes as you wish.

The doll's clothing is up to you. This doll is about 18 in. long, roughly the size of a newborn, so she may wear infant clothes. Clothing with snaps or buttons or elasticized waistbands makes it easier for a child to dress the doll. She is photographed here in a dress once worn by my youngest daughter, Martha.

Bibliography

Historical information relevant to American childhood and folk toys has been taken from many sources; the most important are:

Bell, R. C. *The Boardgame Book.* New York: Exeter Books, n.d.

Calvert, Karin. *Children in the House: The Material Culture of Early Childhood, 1600-1900.* Boston: Northeastern University Press, 1992.

Davis, Glenn. *Childhood and History in America.* New York: The Psychohistory Press, 1976.

deMause, Lloyd. "The Evolution of Childhood," in *The History of Childhood,* ed. Lloyd deMause (pp. 1-74). New York: The Psychohistory Press, 1974.

Durant, Will and Ariel. *Rousseau and Revolution.* New York: Simon and Schuster, 1967.

Edwards, Jonathan. "The Great Awakening," in *The Works of Jonathan Edwards,* Vol. IV, ed. C. C. Goen. New Haven: Yale University Press, 1972.

Erikson, Erik H. *Toys and Reasons: States in the Ritualization of Experience.* New York: Norton, 1977.

Fraser, Antonia. *A History of Toys.* London: George Weidenfeld and Nicholson, 1966.

Greven, Philip J. *The Protestant Temperament: Patterns of Child Rearing, Religious Experience, and the Self in Early America.* Chicago: University of Chicago Press, 1988.

———. *Spare the Child: The Religious Roots of Punishment and the Psychological Impact of Physical Abuse.* New York: Vintage, 1992.

Jackson, F. Neville (Mrs.). *Toys of Other Days.* 1908. Reprint Bronx, N.Y.: Benjamin Blom, 1968.

Jensen, Gerald E. *Buildings in Miniature.* Radnor, Pa.: Chilton, 1982.

Ketchum, William C., Jr. *Toys and Games.* New York: Cooper-Hewitt Museum, 1981.

Nelson, John A. *52 Weekend Woodworking Projects.* New York: Sterling, 1991.

O'Brien, Richard. *The Story of American Toys from the Puritans to the Present.* New York: The Abbeville Press, 1990.

Scarne, John. *Encyclopedia of Games.* New York: Harper and Row, 1973.

Schnacke, Dick. *American Folk Toys: How to Make Them.* Baltimore: Penguin, 1974.

Sutton-Smith, Brian. *Toys as Culture.* New York: Gardner Press, 1986.

Wishy, Bernard. *The Child and the Republic: The Dawn of Modern American Child Nurture.* Philadelphia: University of Pennsylvania Press, 1968.

Photo Credits

p. 4: Courtesy Pocumtuck Valley Memorial Association, Memorial Hall Museum, Deerfield, Massachusetts; photo by Amanda Merullo.

p. 5, top: © The British Museum, London.

p. 5, middle: Courtesy The Metropolitan Museum of Art, Rogers Fund, 1940. (40.2.1)

p. 5, bottom: Courtesy The Metropolitan Museum of Art, The Cesnola Collection; purchased by subscription, 1874-1876. (74.51.815)

p. 7: Courtesy Worcester Art Museum, Worcester, Massachusetts; gift of Mr. and Mrs. Albert W. Rice.

p. 8: Courtesy Worcester Art Museum, Worcester, Massachusetts; Eliza S. Paine Fund in memory of William R. and Frances T. C. Paine.

p. 9: Courtesy University of Pennsylvania Press.

p. 10: Courtesy Pocumtuck Valley Memorial Association, Memorial Hall Museum, Deerfield, Massachusetts; photo by Amanda Merullo.

p. 11, top: Courtesy Peabody Essex Museum, Salem, Massachusetts; photo by Richard Merrill.

p. 11, bottom: Courtesy Germanisches Nationalmuseum, Nuremberg.

p. 12, top: Courtesy Pocumtuck Valley Memorial Association, Memorial Hall Museum, Deerfield, Massachusetts; photo by Amanda Merullo.

p. 12, bottom: Photo by Scott Phillips.

p. 13, top: Courtesy Hadley Farm Museum, Hadley, Massachusetts; photo by Stan Sherer.

p. 13, bottom: Courtesy Historic Deerfield, Inc.; photo by Amanda Merullo.

p. 14: Courtesy Historic Deerfield, Inc.; photo by Amanda Merullo.

p. 15, top left and bottom: Photos by Scott Phillips.

p. 15, top right: © Collection of The New York Historical Society.

p. 16, top and bottom: Courtesy Hadley Farm Museum, Hadley, Massachusetts; photos by Stan Sherer.

p. 17: Photo by Scott Phillips.

p. 18, top: Courtesy Hadley Farm Museum, Hadley, Massachusetts; photo by Stan Sherer.

p. 18, bottom: Courtesy Peabody Essex Museum, Salem, Massachusetts.

p. 19: Courtesy Peabody Essex Museum, Salem, Massachusetts.

p. 20: Photo by Scott Phillips.

pp. 22-49: All photos by Stan Sherer.

pp. 51-165: All photos by Boyd Hagen, except those on pgs. 78, 86, 92, 107, 158, and 161, which are by Scott Phillips, and on p. 148, which is by Stan Sherer.

Book Publisher: Jim Childs

Acquisitions Editor: Rick Peters

Publishing Coordinator: Joanne Renna

Editor: Peter Chapman

Designer: Susan Fazekas

Illustrator: Vincent Babak

Typeface: Garamond

Paper: Warren Patina Matte, 70 lb.

Printer: R. R. Donnelley, Willard, Ohio